PRODUCTIVITY
IMPROVEMENT
MANAGEMENT

BIALEK'S PRODUCTIVITY LAW

Jacques Bialek

CALIFORNIA MANAGEMENT PRESS
SAN FRANCISCO

CALIFORNIA MANAGEMENT PRESS

New Address:
236 West Portal Avenue   Suite 114
San Francisco, CA 94127-1423

PRODUCTIVITY
IMPROVEMENT
MANAGEMENT

BIALEK'S
PRODUCTIVITY LAW

Manufactured in the United States of America

California Management Press
110 Pacific Avenue, Suite 220
San Francisco, CA 94111

Cover design by Shirley Wong

Library of Congress Cataloging in Publication Data

Bialek, Jacques.
    Productivity improvement management.

    Includes index.
    1. Industrial productivity--Management.
    I. Title.
HD56.B49   1987   658.5   87-6557
ISBN 0-941883-01-9 (pbk.)

First Edition

This book is dedicated to my son, Dr. William S. Bialek, theoretical biophysicist teaching at the University of California, Berkeley. He reviewed my early lecture drafts, directed me to the science references I was seeking, helped me place the proper emphasis on the ideas I was trying to put across, and prevented a big mistake in the way I was explaining misconceptions in productivity improvement management.

For this book, as well as for current projects, Bill's tremendous output of research papers is an incentive to get me going—whenever my own productivity is slowing down.

ERRATA

p. 28, line 4. Read "fuel is" for "fuel in".

p. 29, line 19. Read "more effective than" for "more effective that".

p. 55, line 13. Read "resource" for "rsource".

p. 66, line 20. Read "1957" for "1959".

p. 89, line 20. Read "which can do more" for "which can do do more".

p. 136, line 7. Read "by a union" for "by an union".

p. 245, line 11. Read "setting where" for "setting were".

p. 274, line 10. Read "that work led me" for "that work let me".

p. 318, line 23. Read "actual work to be done" for "actual work do be done".

NEW ADDRESS

CALIFORNIA MANAGEMENT PRESS
236 West Portal Avenue, Suite 114
San Francisco, CA 94127-1423

PREFACE

To paraphrase a famous author quoted in this text:

"Why sit through another seminar when
all the information I need is in the book?"

After preparing a management training course, the volume of my notes indicated enough material for a book. I wrote it.

Why did I retain the "lecture" format? Years of teaching experience make me aware of the greatest problem faced while explaining difficult concepts: Keeping the students awake. The "lecture" style allows for more lively explanations than a textbook format. Many productivity concepts are, indeed, complex.

In the text I explain many times why a "canned" or "packaged" approach to productivity improvement should be avoided: What worked at one time in one situation may not work, or be detrimental in another. A "Proven Ways to Improve Productivity" book style would be a costly hoax, even if all the advice is based on successful experience.

The aim of this book is to provide management with more insight on productivity, on the multiple problems to be faced in order to achieve improvement. And, incidentally, to publicize the sometimes startling results of my research, summarized in the "productivity laws."

The reader, or student of this book should gain a

greater awareness of the productivity improvement task, the tools available to tackle it, the initiation and management of a program.

A few of my case histories found at the end of this text indicate that no investment has a greater rate of return than productivity improvement, since many improvements providing immediate problem solution or long range savings cost nothing, except the time of the person who figured it out.

Please make yourself comfortable, relax, and start reading.

CONTENTS

LECTURE 4

PRODUCTIVITY:
RESOURCES AND RESOURCE FACTORS

LECTURE 5

PRODUCTIVITY:
OUTPUTS AND OUTPUT FACTORS

LECTURE 6

PRODUCTIVITY:
IMPROVEMENT PROGRAM ACTION

LECTURE 7

PRODUCTIVITY: IMPROVEMENT MANAGEMENT PRINCIPLES

SUPPLEMENT

LECTURE   1

PRODUCTIVITY: FICTION, FACTS,   AND   POLITICS

SUMMARY:
United States prosperity and leadership depends on national productivity. Political and media statements about productivity are misleading. Three significant economic trends. Our changing economy requires new productivity considerations. Major productivity challenges and opportunities.

INTRODUCTION

Ladies and Gentlemen:

This lecture is an introduction, to give definitions, and to present an overview of productivity at the national level.

For any educational process, the question arises: Should a program be limited to "how to" topics, or be extended to broader aspects of the subject? Within this audience, there are probably people capable of debating the question for many hours.

Anyway, I do feel that discussing some of the general aspects of productivity will set a useful framework for further lectures—and give you a chance to get used to my accent.

Then, since the human mind works in mysterious and wonderful ways, one can never tell—how one sentence, one word, can trigger an idea, a constructive and applicable thought.

So, let us talk about

PRODUCTIVITY, ITS FACTS, FICTION, AND POLITICS

Karl Marx—believed—that the output of industry is entirely the result of Labor.

Of course, such a notion, at this time, is obsolete.

Many people—believe—that productivity depends mostly on Labor, on workers.

Such a notion, at this time, is obsolete, and I will explain why later.

Now, why is there so much public misinformation about such an important issue, affecting all of us, since political decisions, and Government policies are formulated on the basis of trends in national productivity?

One possible reason is, that the figure always quoted is the national change rate in Labor productivity, meaning the percentage change in the value of Gross National Product resulting from one—average—hour of work.

Publicizing this one economic measure is a help in maintaining the belief that productivity depends mostly on Labor, which may have been true fifty years ago, but is not at this time, and I will prove it to you.

The most comprehensive study on the national economic aspects of productivity was reprinted in 1975 as a 630-page book titled "PRODUCTIVITY TRENDS IN THE UNITED STATES," by George W. Kendrick, Professor of Economics at the George Washington University, and the most prolific writer in the nation on productivity.

In the book introduction titled "Basic Facts on Productivity Change," Solomon Fabricant, Director of Research of the National Bureau of Economic Research, whose staff included, at publication time, people like Arthur F. Burns, and Milton Friedman, states:

"Productivity has been much discussed in recent years, and too often misunderstood."

"Productivity deserves the attention it has received, because it is a measure of the efficiency with which resources are converted into commodities and services that men want. Higher productivity is a means of better levels of economic well-being and greater national strength. Higher productivity is a major source of the increment in income over which men bargain and sometimes quarrel. And higher—or lower—productivity affects costs, prices, profit, output, employment, and investment, and thus plays a part in business fluctuations, in inflation, and in the rise and decline of industries."

You will agree that this is a well phrased statement, confirmed by economic developments of the past few years.

Also, note that I am not the first one to realize that productivity is often misunderstood, as stated in two more lines of that introduction:

"Despite its importance and the wide attention paid it, productivity is a subject surrounded by considerable confusion."

PRODUCTIVITY DEFINITIONS

At this point, I must define three technical words used by economists.

OUTPUT: Can mean the Gross National Product of the United States, or the Gross Sales of a corporation.

INPUTS: Are what it takes to produce the OUTPUT, such as Labor, Materials, Equipment, Capital, etc.

Each INPUT is one **FACTOR** contributing to the OUTPUT.

TOTAL FACTOR PRODUCTIVITY: Accounts for all INPUTS.

Now, from the introduction by the author, George W. Kendrick, a paragraph titled "The Productivity Concept."

"The term 'productivity' is generally used rather broadly to denote the ratio of any or all associated inputs, in real terms. Ratios of output to particular inputs may be termed 'partial productivity measures,' the most common of which is output per man-hour.

Partial productivity ratios, while useful for measuring the saving in particular inputs achieved over time, do not measure over-all changes in productive efficiency, since they are affected by changes in the composition of input."
End of quote.

The productivity figures publicized by the news media refer to the changes in national output per man-hour average, obtained by dividing the Gross National Product, in Dollars, by the gross national hours of labor.

This is a "partial productivity ratio," which, to quote Professor Kendrick again, "does not measure over-all changes in productive efficiency."

ORGANIZATION PRODUCTIVITY

Talking of productivity at the national level is a rather abstract exercise. So, let us take an example easy to picture.

Suppose you want to purchase a manufacturing company, and you ask an industrial business broker to find one for you. In the meantime, you have learned the value of productivity. You know that when productivity in a company goes up, profit goes up.

OK. The business broker comes back with two manufacturing companies meeting your purchase price.

Both companies have the same sales volume.

For the purpose of my demonstration, let us ignore the many factors entering into the valuation of a business, and look at productivity only.

The first company has a labor force of 500 employees. The second company, which has been recently auto-mated, requires 50 employees only.

On the basis of productivity, would you buy the second company, since the sales per employee is ten times better than for the first one?

For our evaluation, we will use a simple formula, very helpful for understanding the practical concepts of productivity and productivity improvement—in the case of an organization, such as—a company, a department, a project, etc.

ORGANIZATION PRODUCTIVITY = OUTPUT / RESOURCES

(The organization productivity equals output divided by resources.)

With our manufacturing companies, OUTPUT is the sales volume. RESOURCES include the cost of Labor, materials, equipment, the cost of capital, and all other costs required to produce the OUTPUT.

Looking back at the two business opportunities, using the Labor "partial measure of productivity," would indicate that productivity in the company with 50 employees is ten times higher that in the company with 500 employees, since OUTPUT is the same for both companies.

Of course, such a productivity evaluation, which I have seen in print, is nonsense, because Labor is but one part, one element of the RESOURCES used to produce the company's OUTPUT.

In the factory with 50 employees, the cost of automation is one element of RESOURCES. Suppose the cost of automation was excessive, then the company with 500 employees will generate better earnings, because it has a higher organization productivity.

With a few exceptions, such as comparing two organizations where all conditions are equal, speaking of productivity in terms of worker productivity is meaningless, unless we are talking about ancient industrial history.

Worker productivity is only one part—of the total productivity of an organization. This fact has been known and stated by economists for a long time. However, it does not come through to the public, and the news media is no help, to say the least.

At the national level, one conceptual error is distorting all economic figures related to productivity, because one factor is ignored. We can call it the "idleness factor."

Suppose we are looking at the productivity of a manufacturing plant set up with machines and equipment for 800 employees. With 800 employees working, the plant has a given productivity. Now, suppose that due to bad business conditions, 400 employees only are working in the plant. The company still has to pay for the cost of all idle machines and equipment. This reduces the real overall productivity of the manufacturing plant.

At the national level, the figures entering productivity statistics come from activities, such as value of goods sold, hours worked, etc. Idle plant capacity, unemployed workers, are ignored. Yet, the nation has to pay for idle plants written off the books of a corporation, the nation has to pay for the cost of unemployment.

The wealth of a nation, the standard of living of its citizens, does depend on national productivity. But we must forget the simplistic concept of productivity, such as looking at the worker only. At the business level, at the national level, we must look at all aspects of productivity, and formulate improvement policies accordingly.

GOVERNMENT REGULATION AND PRODUCTIVITY

Now, it is time to talk about another topic which has generated much public misinformation: The relationship between government regulation and productivity.

Because the words "regulation" and "productivity" have entered the current political rhetoric, I would like to emphasize that I have absolutely no political connection, or ambition.

Now, it would be nice if we lived in a society with no need for government regulations. In the meantime, what would you do—if one block away from your home, somebody builds a noisy industrial plant, or an all-night discotheque?

To prevent such occurrence, there are laws, and regulations—enforced through the issuance of permits.

Requiring a permit is good. Six months to process a permit is bad.

Therefore, while there are, without any doubt, abuses and need for reform in government regulation, I find that some people tend to confuse regulation—with the administration of regulation.

> Many sectors of industry complain loudly about government regulation. The most interesting case in point is probably the automobile industry.

I remember the Chairman of the Board of Ford, testifying in Congress against the seat belt regulation. His argument was—that seat belts will increase the retail price of a car by $50—that the price increase will result in reduced car sales, with dire consequences for the American economy.

Seat belts became standard equipment on all domestic makes on January 1, 1964. At that time, new car sales were approximately 8 million units per year. In subsequent years, the figure went up to over 12 million units, a sales increase of 50%.

The punch line to the seat belt regulation story is that in 1981, General Motors started to publish full-page ads in national magazines, explaining why automobile drivers and passengers should use seat belts. Then, Ford—within 2-page magazine spreads started in April 1982, stated: "Seat belts save lives—buckle up."

Finally, on December 5, 1983, I heard an amazing item on television news: General Motors and Ford have requested the United States Government to make the use of seat belts mandatory!

One notable argument given by automobile manufacturers against other regulatory requirements, such as emission standards, is that it reduces productivity!

If you look at the organization productivity formula, the ratio OUTPUT/RESOURCES, you will see that such an argument is contrary to a basic principle of arithmetic.

It is true, that to equip a car with an emission cleaning device requires an increase in RESOURCES: More hours of work, and more materials. If this was the end of the story, of course, productivity would be reduced. But you can be sure—that every time a car requires more labor and materials, the value of the OUTPUT goes up also, because the sales price is increased. Therefore, organization productivity is not affected.

ENGINEERING EFFICIENCY

There is one more important aspect of the relationship between regulation and productivity: Engineering efficiency.

In general, when a machine, an industrial process—is well engineered—it will produce little waste, and be safe, thus meeting any regulatory requirements.

For example, a few years ago, Maserati exported a car to the Unites States meeting all emission standards—without any smog control equipment. The secret was an efficient engine, transforming more gasoline into mechanical energy, instead of wasting it into polluting emission.

I would not want to give the impression that I have a better opinion of foreign automotive engineering. Being an engineer myself, I can tell that there are no major secrets in the engineering of a consumer product: What one company can do, another can do also. Furthermore, the United States does have great resources in engineering research, education, and talent. However, at least in the automotive industry, engineers do not make the top management decisions.

Engineering efficiency, characterized by a good utilization of resources, and avoidance of waste, is one important factor in productivity.

Pollution, dumped garbage, are evidence of waste.

For example, when the late Prime Minister of the Soviet Union, Nikita Krushchev, during his 1959 tour of the United States, visited a farm in Iowa, he discovered that corn husks are processed into livestock feed, while in Russia, it was disposed off as garbage. Krushchev immediately issued appropriate orders to his staff.

To extend the point, here is one actual case history showing how government regulation can be an opportunity to increase industrial productivity.

One factory, in the chemical industry, was heavily polluting the air. When new air pollution regulations went into effect, the company was faced with the decision to either make a substantial capital investment to clean up smokestack emissions, or close the factory.

One characteristic of the processing done in that factory was a high percentage of production costs required for fuel, to produce heat—eventually sent out through the smokestack, together with the pollutants.

Well, the company engineers designed a filtering system incorporating heat exchangers, thus using previously lost heat—to preheat the raw materials.

By the way, this took place during the first major oil crisis of the 70's, when the cost of fuel went up drastically in a short period of time.

Now, here are the results of that management action, followed by the implementation of sound principles of engineering efficiency.

1. The air quality standards were met.

2. Because of the savings in fuel, the filtering system costs were amortized in 2 years, a very short time for a capital investment.

3. Because fuel in an important component of production costs, the company was able to improve its competitive position—and increase its share of the market.

> This is one case—where government regulation—gave company management a kick in the pants, for their own good and profit.

It should not be that way, because in general, any industrial process which has gone unchanged for a long period of time, is obsolete—from the standpoint of productivity.

The same statement can be made about nonindustrial work processes, such as accounting or administrative procedures, the handling of any paperwork.

The reason why industrial and other processes become obsolete, is that advances in technology provide improved equipment, improved materials, improved work methods.

Proper utilization of such improved resources results in improved productivity.

Without loosing sight of productivity, it is to the benefit of industrial and other managements—to keep in mind the commonplace saying that "times are changing."

A negative attitude is to fight change, and it can be profitable, for a while.

A positive attitude is to look at change as an opportunity to do better.

One illustration came to mind, as I was listening to Governor Lee Dreyfus, of Wisconsin, making a major address on the energy crisis, at the Commonwealth

Club of California.

One way to reduce the economic drain caused by the foreign oil imports, is to draw on the coal reserves available in the United States.

The first reaction of potential industrial coal users was: "OK, but government agencies will have to accept more air pollution resulting from the burning of coal."

During his address, Governor Dreyfus gave a plug to the Allis-Chalmers Corporation, located in Wisconsin, who developed a process using coal—with more efficiency than traditional burning methods—while producing less pollution than required by any government regulation.

One last example, to prove the same point:

The ban on DDT, generated a persistent public relations campaign, aimed at eliminating that regulation.

Well, some time ago, European chemical companies have started to manufacture a new insecticide, developed in England, which is 100 times more effective that DDT—therefore requires very small quantities, and is safe for people and livestock.

A person independent of any special interest group, must conclude that regulation, a multifaceted problem, has become, unfortunately, a political issue.

As usual, people with strong opinions for or against any aspect of the issue—tend to ignore purpose, goals, or even the definition of goals, and tend to rely on a very narrow analysis of economic conditions.

It may be productive, for people seeking political office, or gain for a specific interests group, to simplify extremely complex issues, such as regulation.

Unfortunately, economic and societal problems—are

not getting simpler.

It may be time to face the reality: That old-fashioned political concepts cannot deal with the increasing complexity of local, national, and world problems.

Please keep in mind that I am not talking politics, but productivity, although at a level different from the usual Labor connotation.

On that basis, it may be time, to consider solving our mounting problems with the reasonable—and proven concepts of productivity improvement.

NATIONAL PRODUCTIVITY TRENDS THREE MAJOR FACTS

National productivity trends should be of concern to every person, because the nation's standard of living is related to national productivity.

For an analysis of the national aspects of productivity, we would have to look at many U.S. economic trends, such as Gross National Product, Employment, etc. Except that it would get us lost into too many statistical figures. So, I will keep it down to the most relevant facts only.

Three major facts dominate the productivity picture in the United States.

FIRST FACT—AMERICAN AGRICULTURE

The first important productivity fact is—the great productivity success story of American agriculture.

In 1869, 46% of the United States working population, including proprietors, worked in agriculture.

In 1929, it was 20%.

In 1969, 4.3%, and

in 1980, 3.1%.

The remarkable employment distribution trend for agriculture, confirms well the first statement I made today: "It is not true that productivity depends—mostly, on workers!"

Neglecting the effect of imports and exports, it is obvious—that in the past 30 years or so—5 times less people supplying the agricultural needs of the United States is not the result of farmers and their employees working 5 times faster! It is the result of improved equipment, of scientific and engineering achievements, of increased education.

A few years ago, I heard a University of California at Davis Professor, telling that their freshman class in oenology has over 100 students! If California had to wait for people to learn in the family winery, like in the old days, the State would not have the fastest growing wine production and sales—in the world.

SECOND FACT—AMERICAN TOTAL FACTOR PRODUCTIVITY

The second important productivity fact of the American economy, is the tremendous increase in Total Factor Productivity of the Private Sector, which amounted to 134% between 1929 and 1969.

What happened since 1969? The rate of increase in productivity slowed down, then, for the 10-year period between 1973 and 1982 it was, on the average, less than 1%.

In 1983, Private Sector productivity increased by a strong 2.9%, and it is expected to keep growing at an annual rate of about 2.5% for the next few years.

Some people have a simple explanation for the past United States productivity slow down. However, at least a dozen economic research studies I have read on the subject lead to no solid conclusion.

I wish people making assured economic statements on television, would indicate—how difficult it is to substantiate their pronouncements.

REMARKS ON NATIONAL PRODUCTIVITY DATA

With regard to national productivity data, three important points have to be made:

1. United States productivity levels are still higher than those of its Japanese and European competitors. However, for the past few years, productivity

rate increases in those countries have been higher than in the United States, which means that they are closing in on the United States productivity lead.

2. Arriving at national productivity figures is very difficult, because some basic data necessary to compute productivity is obtained through sampling, or is not available. The bottom line is, in my opinion, that a 1% change in national productivity is meaningless, because measurement error is probably higher than 1%.

3. We must keep in mind that national figures are lumping together a great diversity of productivity situations—from the company which had no budget for plant modernization in the past fifty years, to the company investing most of its earnings in new product research, in new plant facilities and equipment.

THIRD FACT
TREND TO SERVICE ECONOMY

The third and most important productivity fact is also, probably the most important trend of the U.S. economy: For many years, the Services Sector makes up over 50% of the Gross National Product.

Leading economists do have different interpretations of the economic data published by the Labor and Commerce Departments. However, with regard to Services, there is no doubt as to the historical trend picture.

Professor Kendrick's Services Sector figures are, for 1969, 53% of the Gross National Product, and 58% of the total U.S. employment.

The March 1981 issue of Scientific American magazine includes a very interesting study titled "The Service Sector of the U.S. Economy," by Eli Ginzberg, Professor Emeritus of Economics at Columbia University, and George J. Vojta, Executive Vice-President of Citicorp / Citibank.

The authors estimate that in 1978, the Services Sector accounted for 66% of the Gross National Product, while Services employment accounted for 68% of the total U.S. employment.

The Scientific American article subtitle states, with regard to the Services Sector:

"It is now the dominant sector, replacing the goods-producing sectors. Other changes are growth of the nonprofit sector, the increase in human capital, and the further internationalization of the economy."

Not everyone may agree with the principles used by

the authors to construct their data. However, there is no doubt that the concluding paragraph of the article does deserve much thought:

"The proposed re-industrialization of an economy dominated by services is an exercise in futility. Americans must unshackle themselves from the notion, dating back to Adam Smith, that goods constitute wealth, whereas services are nonproductive, and ephemeral. At the same time, they should act on Smith's understanding that the wealth of a nation depends on the skill, dexterity and knowledge of its people."
End of quote.

One more point should be made about the shift of the U.S. economy towards a Services economy:

Whatever figures, whatever ratios of Services Gross Product and Employment one accepts—should be increased, because a significant percentage of persons working in the other Sectors of the economy, such as Industry, are, in fact, Service employees within their companies.

FOUR MAJOR PRODUCTIVITY CHALLENGES

Now that we have the basic facts, the most significant trends, what are the great challenges, and the great opportunities for productivity in the United States?

I see four major productivity challenges.

FIRST CHALLENGE OUR OWN ORGANIZATION

The first challenge is to increase productivity in our own organizations, without worrying about national or international trends, without waiting for Washington to decide on new economic legislation—which may help national productivity—a few years from now.

SECOND CHALLENGE
MANAGEMENT

The second challenge is the willingness, the courage, to take a fresh look at the very concepts of management.

For a long time, American management was a model for the Western world. For example, when I was in France, if something wrong happened in an industrial company, one reaction from company executives, I heard many times, was: "This would never happen in the United States. 'They' know how to manage. 'They' know how to organize."

Of course, when I came to the United States, I found that similar organizations, under similar circumstances, experience exactly the same management problems.

Now, in light of the poor performance of some industrial sectors of the United States, and of the success of some sectors of the foreign competition, one may wonder if the time has come to consider changes in management thinking.

Areas I feel well worth looking at are:

— The administrative processes in large organizations.
— The response to change in technology, to change in the economy, to change in society.
— Traditional concepts of business planning, traditional concepts of employee relations.
— The principle of standardized—management and other policies—in view of the increasing diversification of activities, within industrial and service organizations.

It is difficult to generalize and rank the importance of each factor influencing the productivity of an organization. With one exception, the most important factor in all circumstances: Management.

This too, is well worth thinking about.

A good part of my next lecture titled:

"PRODUCTIVITY: NEW MANAGEMENT CONCEPTS" explores the relationship between important aspects of management and productivity in contemporary organizations—a fact which is too often either ignored, or underestimated.

THIRD CHALLENGE
GOVERNMENT

The third major productivity challenge is none other than productivity in government.

There are two aspects to that challenge.

First, government "Management Productivity," meaning the ability of a government—Federal, State, or Local, to fulfill its goals, to solve the problems under its jurisdiction.

Looking at the past twenty or thirty years, the record is generally dismal, the productivity trend—negative. This situation is not exclusive to the United States. Every country of the Western World, more or less, sooner or later, experiences similar problems. In the Eastern World, problems may be different, but the ability of governments to achieve improvement is just as bad.

Having studied management productivity problems both in private enterprise and in government, I can say that both situations are fundamentally related. However, arriving at solutions for government is much more difficult. It is, therefore, a greater challenge.

The second aspect of productivity in government is that of government administration.

I would like to address this topic, because it relates to many years of my professional experience. However, this would take one hour. So, I will condense it into two short statements.

To reduce government expenditures, the "meat axe" approach is the easiest and the fastest. It is also the worse approach, because it results in immediate reduction in government services.

Improving the productivity of government administration and services is difficult, and takes time. But it is the best approach, because it results in permanent reductions of budget and expenditures without reduction in government services.

Based on my experience, I can state, emphatically, that it can be done.

FOURTH CHALLENGE
BASIC SCIENCE

The fourth major productivity challenge is never mentioned, although it represents, by far, the greatest opportunity: This is the challenge of basic science.

Closely related, is the challenge of science and engineering education, which may have received more attention for the engineering part, although its impact on national productivity may not be fully appreciated.

The connection between basic science and productivity improvement is not obvious. There are reasons, easier to explain with two specific examples.

THE LASER

(Light Amplification by Stimulated Emission of Radiation)

The LASER is a great new tool offering countless opportunities for productivity improvement.

In medicine, it allowed the simplification of difficult procedures, with increased safety, and quicker patient recovery. In industry, it allows the performance of basic manufacturing processes, such as cutting, with unprecedented precision. Many industrial automated processes would have been impossible—without the LASER, and new applications are still developed. For example, computer LASER printers can be at least ten times faster than any other type of computer printer, are changing the concepts and reducing the cost of typography.

The U.S. market for LASER scanners used in supermarket check-out, and in industrial applications, was $325 millions for 1982, and is estimated to grow to $1 billion within a few years.

There is some controversy as to who invented and built the first LASER. This was done in the United States, between 1961 and 1963. Then, it took another 5 to 10 years to develop practical LASER applications.

However, there is no controversy as to who did the basic scientific work which made the LASER possible: None other than Albert Einstein. The basic LASER theory is in the classic Einstein paper titled "On the Quantum Theory of Radiation," published in 1917.

Of course, Einstein was not trying to develop the LASER. He was advancing the knowledge of theoretical physics, thus making it possible to develop the LASER.

With the LASER example, we have 50 years between basic science—and productivity improvement applications, hence the difficulty to recognize the connection.

THE TRANSISTOR

The second example of the connection between basic science and productivity is of major importance, not only for productivity improvement, but for the world economy, because it was the trigger of the current industrial revolution.

I am talking about the TRANSISTOR, major contributor to productivity improvement in the past twenty years, because the TRANSISTOR was the break-through which made it possible to manufacture computers.

Without TRANSISTORS, and its derived technology, a computer with the capabilities of a home computer would cost at least $1 million, and would require several full time employees to keep it going.

At this point, there is not one manufacturing or clerical work process which is not, somehow, affected by computers.

Sometimes, the productivity effect of computers is negative, but this is due to people, not technology.

In December 1980, the General Electric company purchased for $100 million a company specialized in "Computer Aided Design" and "Computer Aided Manufacturing."

Making the announcement to the financial community, Reginald H. Jones, Chairman of General Electric company, stated:

"Productivity improvements are impossible without interactive graphics, computerized numerical control tools and robots. The payoff is $4 or $5 for every Dollar invested."

Of course, this was a sales pitch, but nevertheless an impressive productivity improvement figure.

One other effect of the TRANSISTOR, and its derived products, such as integrated circuits, chips, etc., is the new contribution to the national economy.

Without accounting for the many other TRANSISTOR applications, consider that the 20 top American computer companies had 1985 computer revenue of over $94 billion.

Well, the TRANSISTOR resulted from the work of

three physicists named: Bardeen, Brattain, and Shockley. This historical work was completed at the Bell Laboratories in 1948, and was rewarded with the Nobel Prize.

What Bardeen, Brattain and Shockley did, was to apply, and advance, a new scientific discipline called "SOLID STATE PHYSICS." The foundation of solid state physics, work of Nobel Prize winning physicist Felix Bloch, was released in a scientific paper titled "On the Quantum Mechanics of Electrons in Crystals," published in 1928.

While solid state physics has many applications, for the TRANSISTOR, we have 20 years between basic science and a laboratory device, then another few years for industrial products, and a major effect on productivity.

I gave you two examples showing the relationship between basic science and productivity. The same productivity facts apply to any field of science.

For example, periodically, statistics are released, indicating how many billions of Dollars are lost every year by American business, due to the common cold. Similar statistics of waste could be done for other ailments—we could well do without.

I have heard an American physician of international reputation stating—that his practice of medicine is an art, because the scientific knowledge to do otherwise is not available.

POLITICS OF SCIENCE

For a number of years, the funding situation for science in general, basic science in particular, was bad. In recent years, it has become worse, and threatens to become worse yet.

Fifty years ago, in science, the United States was a secondary power. When a bright graduate student in any scientific discipline wanted to work with a top scientist in the field, he had to go to Europe. After World War II, the trend became reversed.

At this time, while major science centers have mushroomed in many countries—as far as Siberia—the United States may still hold the leadership position in science.

The reason for my opinion is the recent distribution pattern of Nobel Prizes, indicating that major U.S. research universities are prominent science centers, and are still attracting talented scientists from other countries.

However, this bright picture is threatened by the current politics of science, and associated higher education activities, which are—already—affecting American industrial productivity, because the high technology industry is suffering from a shortage of engineers.

EFFECT ON ENGINEERING RESOURCES

What does the shortage of engineers has to do with the productivity challenge of basic science?

The connection is as follows:

An engineering student just graduated with a Bachelor's degree is hired at a salary equivalent or higher to that of a young university professor, and for sure much higher than the salary of a young university research scientist.

To be specific, in June 1982, students just graduated with a Bachelor's degree in Electrical Engineering had job offers with a starting salary of $25,000, while a young Ph.D. able to win a National Science Foundation post-doctoral fellowship could look forward to $14,400 a year.

The results are that few people with a Bachelor's degree are willing to go on to graduate study, and that university faculty abandon teaching for the tremendous increase in income available as they join the ranks of industry.

The number of engineering students admitted in universities has to be limited, and the budget crunch results in obsolete educational equipment not being replaced.

The bottom line is, for the future, and in many instances the present: A lowering of the quality and quantity of scientific research performed in the United States, a shortage of human resources needed by American industry, a lowering of national productivity.

Ladies and gentlemen, I submit to you that the old concepts of capital, of investment, of resources, of national economic wealth, have to be revised, to include brainpower, as one of the most valuable commodities.

Furthermore, regardless how much we believe in private enterprise, we have to recognize that within the private enterprise system, the government has certain responsibilities, certain functions, which could not effectively be duplicated by private business initiative.

One of the recent and much acclaimed scientific success of the United States is the Space Shuttle program (tragic accidents notwithstanding). Imagine NASA scientists and engineers having to write their own grant proposals, or having to apply to private corporations for their funding. This is the situation in basic science activities.

In October 1981, the famous—late—U.C. Berkeley Chemistry Professor Joel Hildebrand, during an interview given on the occasion of his 100th birthday, stated:

> "We need not worry about producing too many top-flight scientists; They make their own jobs, as well as jobs for others. They help to prevent depressions."

The economic status of the United States depends—absolutely, on the progress of productivity in all sectors of the American economy.

One example, one sector of the economy which interacts with many others: It has been established that the economic crisis of the late 1970's, characterized mostly by inflation,unemployment, and stagnant national productivity, started with the energy crisis, in other words the runaway prices of oil.

I submit to you that no energy crisis can be solved by political arguments about related issues, such as air pollution.

> We need a breakthrough, for energy, and for many other economic problem areas.

CONCLUSION

Scientific research, complemented by a vast and resourceful technology structure, has proved to be the great provider of major economic breakthroughs. This, ladies and gentlemen, is the greatest productivity challenge.

I do hope that it will be accepted, because it means nothing less than the opportunity to maintain the United States as the first industrial and economic nation in the world.

Thank you.

LECTURE 2

PRODUCTIVITY: NEW MANAGEMENT CONCEPTS

SUMMARY:
Practical management productivity considerations for contemporary organizations. Productivity misconceptions and opportunities. Useless or dangerous productivity improvement activities. A new concept explains major productivity problems and solutions. The technical/ professional management productivity problem; proven solutions. "No cost" resources for productivity improvement.

INTRODUCTION

Ladies and Gentlemen:

A person good at productivity improvement must be capable to picture and practice—ways different from established traditions.

One tradition is to start a lecture with a story designed to warm up the audience.

Well, I have to start with a statement liable to cool an audience.

Productivity is a difficult topic, because in studying productivity, its problems, its improvement, one is faced with many concepts—some obvious, some abstract or intangible.

Oversimplification, or lack of attention to the many aspects of productivity leads to misconceptions—and to many mistakes.

In some cases, it is relatively easy to picture productivity.

For example, a shop with a small number of people performing a simple task.

In some cases, it is very difficult, if not impossible.

For example, one group of people—tinkering in a new scientific field called "SOLID STATE PHYSICS." Eventually, the group's work results in a little device named "TRANSISTOR," which has a major impact on our economy, and marks the starting point of a new and still developing industrial revolution.

How would you define that working group's productivity?

Now, such difficulties do not mean that we have to give up on productivity—when we are not looking at an assembly line.

On the contrary, because an increasing proportion of the population is working in occupations difficult to define with regard to productivity, such as services, technical, professional, and managerial activities, we have to increase our knowledge of productivity, and—most of all—productivity improvement.

For example, it has been estimated that the Services sector of the U.S. economy amounts now to about 2/3 of the Gross National Product, and national employment—a figure well worth remembering while discussing industrial policies, or proposed legislation related to the improvement of national productivity.

PRODUCTIVITY: WHAT IS IT? HOW IS IT DEFINED?

The usually publicized economic figures are of little use to understand the concepts and implications of productivity, because such figures refer to an average national production, or "OUTPUT," in Dollars, per hour of work.

One logical conclusion, when such figures are quoted, could be that the main factor affecting productivity is the worker.

Nothing could be further from the truth.

To understand productivity, productivity improvement, what makes productivity go up or down, one must think in terms of organization productivity, regardless of size of the organization, from a small group of people, to thousands in a giant organization.

EXAMPLE:

Two machine shops, equipped with automatic machines.

The machines in the old shop can produce 60 parts per hour, while the machines in the new shop can produce 100 parts per hour.

It does not matter how well the workers in the old shop operate and maintain the machines, their organization productivity will never equal what can be achieved in the new shop.

On the other hand, if the machines in the new shop are excessively difficult to keep in running order, or if the new shop does not have a good maintenance program, and—if some conditions create an excessive labor turnover, productivity in the new shop can be lower than in the old shop equipped with the slower machines.

Assuming that productivity depends mostly on the workers, on Labor, is a misconception.

Unfortunately, the media is helping to establish such a misconception.

For example, during a television program, the commentator was explaining why productivity in Japan is higher that in the United States.

To make the point, he showed an assembly line worker in a Japanese automobile plant running to pick up a part, a big piece of metal, then running back to his work station to mount the part on the chassis.

The commentator went on to say that he visited many American automobile plants, and never saw American workers moving that fast.

Well, anyone with the slightest amount of experience in work design—would know—that in an assembly line, a worker should not have to run to pick up parts, one at a time. The parts should be delivered to the work station.

I am not familiar with Japanese humor, but I would not be surprised if that television act was a put-on, because if it is true that national productivity, in Japan, is higher than in the United States, it is certainly not because workers are running in assembly plants.

PRODUCTIVITY
FORMULA-CONCEPT

Rather than defining productivity on a national level, it is more convenient, and useful to think of productivity in terms of a specific organization, such as—a shop, a department, a company, a specific group or activity, a specific project.

This does not mean that the "specific" organization we are talking about is small—but we can picture it, and we can, hopefully, influence its productivity.

The productivity definition of an organization is a ratio, and can be expressed as the total OUTPUT produced by the organization, divided by the RESOURCES used to produce that OUTPUT.

The simple mathematical equation is:

PRODUCTIVITY = OUTPUT / RESOURCES

(Productivity equals output divided by resources.)

OUTPUT, depending on what is more appropriate, or possible to measure, may be expressed as a quantity, such as "300 units per day," or as a Dollar value.

RESOURCES are made up of several components, such as labor, materials, equipment, etc. Again, depending on what is more appropriate, or possible to measure, RESOURCES can be expressed as a quantity, such as units of labor, or as a Dollar value—subject to interpretation, such as the value of capital used to run an organization.

I call this simple productivity equation "FORMULA-CONCEPT" because a detailed economic model of a productivity situation would require a mathematical model, which could be very complex.

Our purpose is not to describe the formulation of economic models, but to explain the concepts of productivity. The simple "formula-concept" fills that purpose.

ORGANIZATION PRODUCTIVITY FORMULA

However, before showing how we can use the organization productivity ratio in a practical and useful manner, I do feel that it is necessary to complicate the formula, slightly, to bring productivity and productivity improvement into the reality of present times.

This will be done by adding the word "FACTOR" to the previous equation, as follows:

PRODUCTIVITY = OUTPUT + OUTPUT FACTORS / RESOURCES + RESOURCE FACTORS

(Productivity equals output plus output factors divided by resources plus rsource factors.)

OUTPUT FACTORS can be difficult to define, or value, such as the quality of a product or service, the good will generated by a company, etc.

OUTPUT FACTORS can be specific to one company, or to one type of organization.

THE NEW SALES MANAGER

This is an actual case I have witnessed, in a company manufacturing industrial products to customer specifications.

A new Sales Manager increased the company sales

by 30%—in a few months—without hiring more sales personnel, or increasing other sales expenditures.

Does this mean that the productivity of the sales department had gone up? In absolute terms, yes.

However, the new Sales Manager's pricing policy was too low, with the result that the company made no profit on the increased sales volume, and of course, looked for a new Sales Manager.

In this case, "profit" was one output factor of major importance, in evaluating productivity improvement in the sales department.

RESOURCE FACTORS are just as difficult to define and value, such as work environment, management know-how, etc.

However, the difficulty in defining, valuing, or even identifying output and resource factors in a given organization is no excuse to ignore the importance of such factors.

THE FAINTING ASSEMBLY LINE WORKERS

For example, with regard to one resource factor, work environment, I have witnessed the case of a large assembly plant in Southern California, where the fumes caused by about one thousand soldering irons were allowed to simply move up to the ceiling, without proper ventilation. On hot days, women were fainting at their work stations.

Eventually, due to working conditions, and other labor relations problems, the plant workers went on a long strike.

The company decided to move out of California.

This is a productivity horror story, which should

never be allowed to happen, even if only the interests of the company stockholders are to be taken into consideration.

There are several other ways to define productivity, although it is always a ratio. However, I feel that the ratio "OUTPUT plus OUTPUT FACTORS" divided by all "RESOURCES plus RESOURCE FACTORS" is the most significant way—to visualize productivity—for the purpose of productivity analysis, and productivity improvement.

While a ratio is a figure, or a number, in the case of a productivity ratio, it means nothing—by itself.

The productivity ratio means something—only if it is used to compare two organizations, or the same organization at different times, or to evaluate what happens, or is liable to happen, when some action is about to be taken with possible effect on productivity.

Of course, changes in the ratio are good causes for management concern, or self-congratulations.

BASIC IMPROVEMENT DEFINITIONS

In practical terms, the meaning and implications of the productivity formula can be applied to define productivity improvement, as follows:

TABLE I   3 WAYS TO ACHIEVE PRODUCTIVITY IMPROVEMENT

	RESOURCES	OUTPUT	POSITIVE OUTPUT FACTORS
(1)	[=]	[+]	[=]
(2)	[-]	[=]	[=]
(3)	[=]	[=]	[+]

TABLE I indicates:

(1) For the same RESOURCES necessary to run the organization, the OUTPUT produced by the organization has been increased.

(2) For the same OUTPUT produced by the organization, the RESOURCES necessary to run the organization have been reduced.

(3) For the same RESOURCES necessary to run the organization, and the same production OUTPUT, positive OUTPUT FACTORS, such as quality, user satisfaction, have been increased.

This third definition of productivity improvement applies in cases where it is difficult, or even impossible to place a Dollar sign, or other quantitative value on the OUTPUT.

For example, a medical service
—as viewed by the patients,

or a government service
—as viewed by the taxpayers.

PRODUCTIVITY FACTORS

The blame for declining national productivity in the United States, is usually placed on "Labor," and on "government regulations."

This is a dangerous view, because it could imply that nothing more can be done to improve productivity, except to "speed up" Labor, and eliminate most government regulations.

My research work has identified, so far, 51 factors affecting productivity.

"Labor," and "government regulations" are but 2 of the 51 factors.

Going into details of all factors affecting productivity would take hours, because each factor must be approached carefully, and treated with lengthy qualifications.

For example, I do have positive evidence that "employee morale" is one factor affecting productivity.

However, many attempts to improve productivity, based on systematic improvement of employee morale—have failed, or even backfired into lower productivity.

The reality is—that most—if not all factors affecting the productivity of an organization interact with each other, in a manner which is unique to that organization.

Hence the danger of oversimplifying the analysis of a productivity situation, the potential disappointment in expecting—that a standard improvement method—will solve a productivity problem likely to be specific to one organization.

PRODUCTIVITY MEASUREMENT

Now, let us talk about one extremely important aspect of productivity and productivity improvement:

The subject of productivity measurement, in its usual, work oriented connotation.

Here is a statement—or a question:

"Productivity must first be measured, in order to be improved?"

Before answering this question, permit me to say that I have years and years of experience in solving productivity problems in many organizational settings, and that I am not the only one to have reached the same conclusion:

"NO, measurement is not the necessary first step for productivity improvement."

Here is a quote from an article on the subject by Gerald Nadler, Professor of Industrial Engineering at the University of Wisconsin, in the March 1978 issue of "Industrial Engineering," the magazine published by the Institute of Industrial Engineers:

> "When—engineers place too much emphasis on measurements, the desired results may not be what expected—and can even be disastrous."

End of quote.

The reason why the most extreme care should be given to—even the consideration of a productivity measurement program, is that it can have a whole range of possible results:

> The best result being an immediate improvement in productivity—even if nothing else is done.

> The worst result is that it can badly damage labor relations—even trigger a strike.

Example: I am now quoting from an article about Safeway stores, published by the financial magazine Forbes, in February 1980.

"New Chairman Magowan complains that Safeway has too many problems with grievances, arbitrations, absenteeism, workers compensation abuses, productivity and strikes, and vows to improve the company's labor relations. A 19-week Teamsters strike hurt Safeway earnings in 1978."

What the Forbes article did not say, is that the strike was triggered by a new measurement program, related to the loading of delivery trucks at the Safeway distribution centers.

> We cannot overemphasize the potentially
> counterproductive effect of actual work
> measurement, or of any action which
> can be interpreted by personnel as being
> a work measurement program.

However, the problems associated with measuring productivity should not prevent productivity improvement activities to go on. In fact, I have verified, many times, that such a course of action is practical—and successful.

While productivity measurement can be difficult, or impossible, or harmful, productivity evaluation, using existing operational data, such as "number of items processed per week," or "quantity produced per day," can—when necessary, provide the answers expected from direct measurement.

During any productivity improvement activity, one danger to be avoided is to let personnel make the assumption—that it is the continuation of what the quote/ unquote "Efficiency Expert" used to do in the old days.

Such an assumption would prevent personnel cooperation, and could make the productivity improvement efforts useless.

In a situation where people are still suspicious about productivity improvement activities, there is an easy way out: Why call it "productivity?"

I have solved many productivity problems without the word "productivity" ever being mentioned. In fact, I have solved many management problems without the word "management" ever being mentioned.

A given "productivity" problem may truthfully be called an "organization" problem, or a "communications" problem, or a "management system" problem, etc.

What really counts, is to solve the problem.

COMPREHENSIVE MANAGEMENT SYSTEM

Now, let us look at one very important productivity concept.

I call it the COMPREHENSIVE MANAGEMENT SYSTEM.

Whenever an organization has a productivity problem, the usual, and perhaps natural tendency is to blame people: Either people doing the work, or a supervisor, or even a top manager. One possible explanation for such a tendency is—that most critics of what an organization is doing, prefer dealing with a tangible concept, such as "the person behind the desk."

The fact is, that COMPREHENSIVE MANAGEMENT SYSTEMS, a concept not readily obvious, are often—either responsible for productivity problems, or for preventing the solution of a productivity problem.

What I call "COMPREHENSIVE MANAGEMENT SYSTEM," as applied to a given organization, includes the principles by which the organization is set up, and—the policies, the procedures, as well as the specific systems used to carry out the work.

The practical aspects of the concept are summarized below.

TABLE II
COMPREHENSIVE MANAGEMENT SYSTEM

COMPREHENSIVE
MANAGEMENT
SYSTEM

ORGANIZATION

POLICIES

PROCEDURES

SPECIFIC
SYSTEMS

There are many situations where the COMPREHEN-
SIVE MANAGEMENT SYSTEM must be studied and
improved—before a productivity problem can be solved.
One such situation is when a new type of activity is
taking place. What I call "new" applies to an activity
different from what it was before, either because of
size, or nature of the work, or circumstances, or any
other consideration.

I shall give you a specific, and famous example of a new activity—and its productivity problem—soon. For size, the general and classic management example is that of a growing company: The COMPREHENSIVE MANAGEMENT SYSTEM for a successful 100-employee company will create productivity problems—if it is still unchanged when the company has 1,000 employees.

For nature of the work, we see it when one company in one line of business absorbs a company in another line of business, and impose its COMPREHENSIVE MANAGEMENT SYSTEM on the purchased company. The purchased company may start loosing money for the first time in its 100-year history—may have to be sold at a loss. This has happened many times in recent years, as corporations moved too fast with their plans for diversification, or in the formation of conglomerates.

EARLY U.S. SPACE PROGRAM

One famous—new—type of management situation did exist when the United States Space Program was started: There was no precedent for such a project, although it was natural to assume that it was an extension of other Department of Defense programs, and could be managed the same way.

With the early United States Space Program, the evidence of low project productivity was with missile launches fizzling over the ocean, or command control pushing the "abort" button, as the missile was turning around and heading in the wrong direction.

The Space Program was going so badly, that President Eisenhower went on television to reassure the public. All he could show, in the way of tangible achievement, was a small missile nose cone—made of a new material capable of withstanding extraordinary changes in temperature, a problem when a missile re-enters atmosphere.

The next morning, I was in a meeting with aero-space industry executives, and there were embar-rassed smiles, when someone asked if we had seen the President holding up a nose cone, during his Space Program progress report to the nation.

Little did we know—that the nose cone was made of "Pyroceram," a new material destined to become a great marketing success, as it entered every American household under the name "Corning Ware."

> Which may prove that productivity is not always as bad—as it can appear to be.

At that time, responsibility for the U.S. Space Pro-gram was spread amongst a number of government agencies, and contractors.

It took the success of "Sputnick," name of the first Russian space mission, which translates to "Co-journeyer," and took place on October 4, 1959, to initiate and implement a new centralized program manage-ment concept—capable of increasing the productivity of this unprecedented type of project.

Managing the U.S. Space Program was done by the newly founded Ramo Wooldridge Corporation. Later on, Ramo Wooldridge merged with its financial backer, the Thomson Corporation, to become "TRW."

> It is not possible—to overemphasize—the direct relationship between COMPREHENSIVE MANAGEMENT SYSTEMS and productivity. In all large organizations I have observed, an inadequate COMPREHENSIVE MANAGE-MENT SYSTEM was not, necessarily, the only, but always a major factor for problems of low

productivity.

Of course, "large organizations" includes government organizations.

We talked about productivity as it relates to COMPREHENSIVE MANAGEMENT SYSTEMS.
It is indeed difficult to talk about productivity without talking about—management.

TECHNICAL MANAGEMENT PRODUCTIVITY

Technical management productivity is a subject of utmost importance for contemporary organizations.

To introduce the concept of technical management productivity, I have to refer to Professor Laurence Peter, who became famous with his best seller titled "The Peter Principle."
The "Principle" is, that in an organization, personnel tend to rise—to their level of incompetence.
Professor Peter arrived at his "Principle" while studying a school system in Canada. He found that outstanding teachers, elevated to school administrative positions, performed badly in their new functions.
Within the context of this lecture, I will call this management performance problem, a problem of management productivity, which, unfortunately, is not lim-

ited to Canadian school systems—or to school systems.

In fact, the extent of management productivity problems is generally underestimated, both in private business and in public agencies.

By no means do I want to challenge Professor Peter's many times verified "Principle," but I do feel that—the way it is phrased—does not reflect completely what is happening—when the outstanding teacher becomes an incompetent administrator.

This is one management problem area I have studied extensively. I call it the TECHNICAL MANAGEMENT PRODUCTIVITY PROBLEM.

I am using the word "technical" for lack of a better descriptive word. Perhaps "professional activities" management would do.

What I mean by "technical" is an activity requiring a high level of specialization—very remote from the "generalist" outlook usually found in good managers.

I first started studying the TECHNICAL MANAGEMENT PRODUCTIVITY PROBLEM when I was working in engineering.

Typically, a good engineer is promoted to a first line supervisory position, where he still does a good job, because most of his time is spent dealing with engineering work.

As the engineer is promoted to higher positions, he has to deal with more and more administrative and management work. This is where the break occurs:

Either the engineer becomes a good manager, or fails at engineering management, thus, apparently, following Peter's Principle.

What is really happening, is that the engineer did not fail at engineering. He or she failed at management—just like the good teacher can fail at school administration.

The basic reason for failure, is that such an engineer really prefers engineering work, over administrative or management work.

THE FAST RISING ENGINEERING EXECUTIVE

For example, I knew the case of an outstanding engineer, who had a meteoric rise through the ranks of a large corporation, until he was promoted to the prestigious position of Corporate Vice-President of engineering.

His door was always open to any company engineer who had to solve a tough engineering problem. Every day, some time during the afternoon, the Vice-President's old buddies will drift into his office, one by one. The whole group will be working hard and well, until late hours.

After six months of such activities, the company President called in the Vice-President of Engineering—to remind him that he is now a Vice-President, and that he is expected to function as a corporate executive.

The Vice-President left the corporation, to take a job with less pay, as Chief Engineer of a small company, where he could spend most of his time doing what he liked best: Engineering.

The technical management productivity problem is liable to occur in most technical, professional, specialized activities.

The problem can affect any type of organization. However, it tends to increase with organization size and complexity—when the management ability at the executive level becomes more important than technical ability.

There are many types of technical management productivity problems. They can be solved.

In general, the solutions, while requiring thorough individual analysis, are within the areas of top management policy, and organization structure.

However, top management must first be willing to recognize that such a problem situation exists, then—management has to be very flexible in the development of appropriate policies.

THE NEW CHIEF ENGINEER

I would like to give you one extreme example, to illustrate the point—of an open-minded and flexible management policy solving a technical management productivity problem.

The President of a small electronics company hired a new Chief Engineer. At first, everything goes smoothly. Then, the new Chief Engineer develops a pattern, whereby he comes to work later and later, while going home later and later.

The company President decides that the situation must be straightened out, and calls in the Chief Engineer—who confesses to a peculiar aspect of his personality, whereby he is much more productive working at night, rather than during the day—and asks the President to let him work that way.

The President decided to give it a try. The work pattern was—that the Chief Engineer would come in about one hour before quitting time, to confer with his staff.   Then, he would work until an unknown hour, sometimes until early shift workers would be coming in.   The company President was a patient man. He had no engineering problems. The work performance of the Chief Engineer resulted in the company increasing its technical reputation—and winning more contracts. The Chief Engineer stayed on the job—working nights.

This was a "flextime" management policy, well ahead of its time.

NEW HIRE AT THE MIT RADIATION LABORATORY

The case of the Chief Engineer most productive while working on the night shift, reminds me of the case of the new hire at the Radiation Laboratory, established at MIT in 1940, essentially to develop Radar, which became a major factor in favor of the allied war effort, during the most difficult period of World War II.

I am now quoting from a New Yorker magazine profile of Isidor Isaac Rabi, who won the Nobel Prize for physics in 1944:

"Julian Schwinger—who had been a Rabi student since 1935, when he was sixteen, was recruited and became a legendary part of the Radiation Laboratory. He worked all night and slept during the day. "At five o'clock, when everybody was leaving, you'd see Schwinger coming in, "Rabi said. I was once told that people would leave unsolved problems on their desks and blackboards, and find when they returned the next morning that Schwinger had solved them. "The problems he solved were just fantastic."

By the way, Schwinger won the Nobel Prize for physics in 1965.

You may wonder why I am referring to work activities taking place in 1940.

It is one example—how—unusual management policies can benefit the productivity of an organization.

But there is more to it. First, let me quote again from the Rabi profile:

"The Laboratory began with about thirty people—mostly nuclear physicists from the universities. It existed for sixty months, at the end of which it had four thousand people."

End of quote.

From both the theoretical and practical aspects of technical management and productivity, the MIT Radiation Laboratory is of great importance. It was, at the time, with four thousand people, the largest scientific and engineering organization ever assembled.

Research I have done on the MIT Radiation Laboratory indicates—that management policies—unprecedented for an organization of that size and scope, were a major factor for the Laboratory's achievements, its output, its extraordinary productivity.

In the late 1950's, I was working at solving management and productivity problems in a Research and Development organization made up of 5,000 people, with a majority of engineers and scientists.

During a meeting with company executives, one Laboratory Director made this statement:

"As far as knowing how to manage such a large Research and Development organization—we are still babes in the woods."
Nobody argued the point.

I have explained the "COMPREHENSIVE MANAGEMENT SYSTEM" concept.

The productivity of technical, professional organizations, depends, to a large extent, on flexibility—with regard to the research, the development, and the implementation of appropriate COMPREHENSIVE MANAGEMENT SYSTEMS.

PRODUCTIVITY AND CHANGE

We have seen how productivity problems do exist with new management situations.
Potential productivity problems exist with any changed management situation.
If an organization is planning to make any type of change, without—first—analyzing the potential effect on productivity, the outcome can be catastrophic.

I have seen it happening many times.

There are two types of changed situations: One that is planned, intentional, and one that just happens.
The latter is more difficult to perceive as a danger to

productivity, because it can set in slowly.

One slow change affecting all organizations is social change.

> Failure of COMPREHENSIVE MANAGEMENT SYSTEMS to respond to the changes taking place in society, either creates productivity problems, or causes to miss opportunities for productivity improvement.

For example, while labor shortage, and turnover—are factors of low productivity, it is not such a long time ago when business, including big business, was missing the opportunity to hire mature, and even not so mature persons eager to re-enter the job market.

Eventually, the population age trend pattern created an acute shortage of young office workers, and business had to hire more mature job applicants.

It did not take long, for large corporations, to advertise, in public relations releases, how smart they were to hire mature ladies, because precise statistical studies proved that they are steady, reliable employees, and—do not take time off to have babies.

> The answer to the "slow" productivity problems settling into an organization—regardless of reason, starts with a periodic, open minded productivity analysis of all aspects of the organization, from top management policy, to mail room activity.

GOVERNMENT RESPONSE TO CHANGE

The counterproductive effect of not recognizing social change applies to government also, and has been, many times, recorded in history. For example, after the end of World War II, European governments failed to realize that the "colonial times" are over. By the time colonies were granted independence, tens of thousand lives had been lost, uselessly.

Well, we could talk about productivity for hours, without exhausting the subject.

We barely touched the subject of productivity improvement. This is the topic of my next lecture, titled "PRODUCTIVITY: THE ELUSIVE GOLD MINE," where I describe the basic requirements and methods for productivity improvement.

RELATIVE PRODUCTIVITY EVALUATION

We looked at many productivity concepts. One more, is the productivity evaluation—of one organizational unit—in relation to a larger unit.

Here is one example of what I mean:

In a large company, one typing group is turning out

statistical reports. By any standard, the productivity of the typing group is high. However, the statistical reports, a pet project of one executive, are really of no use to the company.

From a company standpoint, the value of the typing group's output is zero. Therefore, and in accordance with the simple arithmetic of the organization productivity formula, the typing group's productivity is equal to "ZERO divided by the cost of RESOURCES," in other words—zero.

Productivity evaluations are most informative, or revealing, when it is possible to make a comparison—either between two similar organizations, or for the same organization—at different times.

One well known example of productivity comparison, is Professor Parkinson's analysis of the British Admiralty: He discovered that the number of admirals in the British Navy—had gone up, during the years—in reverse proportion to the number of flagships in service—the largest number of admirals being reached when England had no more flagships on the seas.

"NO COST" IMPROVEMENT RESOURCES

We talked about COMPREHENSIVE MANAGE-
MENT SYSTEMS, a slightly intangible concept,
but nevertheless a major factor in the productivity of an organization.

Because inside and outside conditions affecting an
organization change all the time, concern for productivity requires periodic updating of COMPREHENSIVE
MANAGEMENT SYSTEMS, including top management policy.

In fact, some of my most interesting productivity
problem solving experiences were achieved through a
change in management policy, or in organization
structure. More details later.

The great advantage of productivity improvement accomplished through a change in policy, in organization, or other component of the COMPREHENSIVE
MANAGEMENT SYSTEM, is that—usually—it requires no or negligible investment.

One important point—is—that having a COMPRE-
HENSIVE MANAGEMENT SYSTEM, or any part of
the SYSTEM which does not allow an increase in productivity, or cannot deal with a given productivity problem—is no adverse reflection on the people running the
organization—providing they have the willingness to
implement a new, or modified—better COMPREHEN-
SIVE MANAGEMENT SYSTEM.

CONCLUSION

On a slightly philosophical note, we can say that productivity is one of the most important concepts of civilization, because, regardless of what aspect of human endeavor we are looking at, it characterizes the difference between failure, stagnation, and—achievement, progress.

Then, from a strictly practical standpoint, let us keep in mind that the most important aspect of productivity work:

> Is not—to worry about national economic or political pronouncements.

> Is not—to arrive at statistical figures.

> Is not—to develop productivity measurements.

> Is not—to hand out medals, or dunce caps.

> What really counts—is to increase productivity.

Thank you.

LECTURE 3

PRODUCTIVITY:
THE ELUSIVE GOLD MINE

SUMMARY:
Misleading and obsolete productivity concepts. Major barriers to higher productivity. Requirements to achieve productivity improvement. Research yields unsettling "productivity law." Policies and practices leading to the productivity gold mine.

INTRODUCTION

Ladies and Gentlemen:

Why do I call productivity the "elusive" gold mine?

Because, in many organizations, there are opportunities to improve productivity, except that such opportunities are seldom obvious, and few people sense their existence.

Because, in many instances, productivity improvement can be achieved at no cost at all, a fact difficult to accept.

Because, if an investment is specifically directed at productivity improvement—it will have a rate of return very much higher than any other type of capital investment.

Why is it so difficult to reach that gold mine?

Because there are a number of problems to overcome. To classify such problems as management problems would not be wrong. However, it is only one aspect of the question.

Let me illustrate what I intend to tell you with a short story—about a person, who (probably) had some outstanding management abilities: John D. Rockefeller, the man who built the Standard Oil empire.

THE NEW STANDARD OIL EXECUTIVE

One day, Rockefeller hired a new executive. Let us call him George.

A few weeks later, returning from a trip, Rockefeller stayed in his office until late. On his way home, he noticed a light coming out from one of the executive offices. He walks over, to find out that this is George's office.

John D. enters, and sees George hard at work, behind a desk covered with stacks of paper.

Rockefeller asks: "George, what is going on?"

George, pointing with both hands to the stacks of paper, answers: "There is just a lot of work to be done. I have to stay and work late every day."

John D. shook his head. Then, pointing at the stacks of paper:

"George, I did not hire you to do THAT!"

"If you have too much work, hire an assistant. Then, after you have cleared your desk, I want you to lean back on your chair, put your feet up, relax—and—

"THINK UP SOME NEW WAYS TO MAKE MONEY!"

This short story illustrates one major problem preventing the understanding, and therefore the improvement of productivity.

The problem is—that people make assumptions about productivity.

The origin of such assumptions could probably be explained, but it would be of little use.

Well, one such assumption is—that high productivity is directly related to hard work.

The next, and almost universal extension of this assumption, is to equate the 'appearance' of hard work with real high productivity.

WORK AND PRODUCTIVITY

The fact is, as far as one person's work output is concerned, that high productivity results—mostly—from smart work, not from hard work.

Apparently, John D. Rockefeller knew it, and it did not hurt his business.

Closer to our times, here are a few lines printed in 1972. Three short quotes:

"—the aim of the continuing productivity effort today—is not to get people to work harder, but to work smarter."

"Notice that in all our improvement, workers involved are not required to work any faster. No speedup is involved. In fact, work has been simplified."

"—you don't basically improve productivity by making a person work harder or faster."

The quotes are from three lectures on Productivity Improvement, by Donald C. Burnham, who was, at the time, Chairman and Chief Executive Officer of Westinghouse.

Sometimes, I wonder how much progress has been made with regard to the "hard work" assumption.

Of course, when I started to become interested in the problems of management, of productivity, I remember some old timers—businessmen, who divided people into two categories only: The hard workers—and the others.

In order to make that evaluation, they would look at the palms of a man's hands: If the skin was rough, the man was a "real" worker. If the skin was smooth—well, assuming that the man was working, the poor fellow had to be a bookkeeper, or perhaps an engineer, who, in accordance with the same type of thinking, had his drafting table standing in the least desirable factory location.

MAJOR FALLACIES

While it is now accepted, I hope, that the condition of a worker's hands mean nothing—with regard to productivity, I wonder how much progress has been made in some of the ways work situations—and workers, are being evaluated.

For example, I have witnessed the same scene thirty years ago, twenty years ago, ten years ago, and even more recently:

> I am walking through a work area with an executive, and he (or more recently she) gets upset because an employee is reading a professional magazine—on company time!

The fact is—that the employee's work output for that day has nothing to do with the few minutes spent looking at the magazine. Furthermore, the employee may get an idea, worth to the company several thousand times the pay received while reading the magazine.

The confusion between the appearance of hard work,

and real productivity, is so well anchored in people's mind, that it was the basis for a book, a best seller, later made into a musical play, and a movie: "How To Succeed In Business Without Really Trying." The book, written by Shepherd Mead, teaches the tricks—that will make upper management believe that an employee is a productive worker, thus insuring promotions up the executive ladder.

There is one type of highly unproductive worker. There is one in—almost—every office. You must have known at least one. He or she, while highly unproductive, succeeds in being highly rated by management.

Typically, during the day, that employee is talking. On the telephone, with visitors, or both. Any matter which should be settled in two minutes stretches into a one hour conference. Of course, by the end of the day, that employee's desk is piled high with things to be done.

When most employees in the office are going home, that employee really gets to work—and will be working late. Executives going home late, may notice that employee, and possibly remark, with satisfaction, that at least, here is one employee who is not afraid of hard work.

By the way, this highly unproductive person is not, necessarily, one of the employees. He or she, is often—an executive.

> **There is no connection between the appearance of hard work and worker productivity.** In other words, there is no connection between the appearance of hard work—and the actual amount and value of work—produced in a given time period.

Unfortunately, the "hard work appearance assumption" is still strongly anchored in a large percentage of the population—including the management population.

For example, if, by no fault of their own, a group of employees find themselves with little to do, their supervisor is likely to tell: "For heavens sake, at least 'look' busy. Imagine the big boss walking by, and seeing you working on a crossword puzzle!"

A quote-unquote "tough" boss may even fire the employee caught doing the crossword puzzle.

A "smart" manager will stop by, and help the employee with a difficult word in the puzzle—then—set out to solve the problem causing this group of employees not to receive a steady flow of work.

When an employee is unproductive, it is an error to assume, automatically, that it is the employee's fault. Firing that employee may satisfy management, and the observers or critics of the organization. It does not necessarily improve the organization's productivity.

My "productive appearance" observations are not new. The French philosopher La Rochefoucauld (1613-1680) wrote: "The world rewards more often the appearance of merit rather than the merit itself."

One of the great pioneers and founders of scientific management, Frank B. Gilbreth, was well aware of the hard work appearance fallacy. Those of you who may not have had the opportunity to study the history of management, may be aware of the book written by one of Gilbreth's daughters, and later made into a delightful movie: "Cheaper By The Dozen." The title refers to the twelve children in the Gilbreth household.

I once had the privilege to sit in a meeting next to Mrs. Gilbreth, then listen to her lecture on management. She was in her eighties, and still active in the consulting firm founded by her husband Frank Gilbreth.

Anyway, at a time when next to nothing was known about industrial management, Frank Gilbreth would tell an incredulous factory owner—that he can increase the production output of his factory—without increasing the number of employees. In other words, increase productivity.

When beginning the consulting engagement, Gilbreth would startle the factory owner, or his shop foreman, with a strange question:

> "Do you have one worker—with a well established reputation for being lazy? I mean the kind of fellow who would rather sit at his bench, than work standing up, who hangs up a tool within reach—to avoid walking over a storage shelf, like everyone else?"

Then, Gilbreth would observe the "lazy" worker's ways, or methods, and use his observations as the basis to establish production methods, to be followed by all workers in the shop. Productivity went up.

While it is difficult to accept that the appearance of hard work—has nothing to do with productivity, it is more difficult to accept that—real hard work has little to do with productivity, or, more specifically, with the positive, useful contribution made to the organization.

While such statements may go against the grain of established thinking—looking at productivity from a strictly management point of view, what counts is the bottom line, the contribution.

It is only an assumption—that the employee working "hard" is a good and productive employee. This is especially true in cases where it is difficult to evaluate work output, or contribution, such as in the case of professional and management employees.

For good measure, let us add the work output of an

elected politician, who knows what pleases the voters, and is always eager to publicize the long hours spent on the job.

PRODUCTIVITY AND POLITICS

The word "politician" leads us into one problem connected with productivity: The problem of generating wrong or misleading opinions about productivity, regardless if this is done for political reasons, or due to the lack of understanding of the very complex conceptual aspects of productivity.

For example, whenever a financial or economic columnist starts lamenting about decreasing productivity rates in the United States, the next paragraph— usually—places the blame on both "Labor" and "Government Regulations."

To address the topic of relationship between Government Regulation and productivity would take up an excessive amount of time. While I will allude to it again, the topic is analyzed in my first lecture titled "PRODUCTIVITY: FICTION, FACTS, AND POLITICS."

PRODUCTIVITY AND MANAGEMENT

As far as blaming lower productivity trends on "Labor," this, again, is an assumption.

First, let me assure you that I have absolutely no political activity, affiliation, or ambition.

Now, let me give you an opinion from a person who

could hardly be suspected of being "pro-Labor": Bob Peterson, President of Iowa Beef Processors (IBP), 1980 sales of $4.6 billion.

IBP came to my attention because it gained first place in the meat packing industry, mostly by improving productivity, in the chain going from cattle on the hoof, to the restaurant or retail meat market.

The statement quoted was printed in the June 22, 1981 issue of Forbes magazine, and I am warning you that the words are a little harsh.

"People who blame the labor unions for this nation's sliding productivity," says IBP President Peterson, "are barking up the wrong tree. Put the blame where it really belongs—on management, which has, by default, forfeited its right to manage."

For a more scholarly opinion—and analysis, I recommend a paper by Professors Robert H. Hayes and William J. Abernathy, titled: "Managing Our Way to Economic Decline," and published in the July-August 1980 issue of the Harvard Business Review.

Also, with reference to the research work reflected in my lecture titled "PRODUCTIVITY: NEW MANAGEMENT CONCEPTS," I have explored the relationship between some important aspects of management and productivity—in contemporary organizations—a fact which is too often either ignored, or underestimated.

MAJOR PRODUCTIVITY IMPROVEMENT EXAMPLE

My observation is—that no major, significant improvement in productivity had ever anything to do with "Labor," "Government Regulations," "hard work," or any other traditional productivity assumption. Here is one example, which should make the point.

I do not know how many of you remember the electromechanical calculator. I do not mean the accounting-type adding machine, but calculators, able to carry out extensive computations.

The machines, made mostly by two companies named Marchant and Friden, were about the size of an office typewriter, and quite noisy.

In the nineteen fifties, such machines were priced around $1,500. Counting for inflation, this will make over $3,000 now—if such machines were still produced. Instead, you can buy, for $30 or less, an electronic calculator which can do do more than the old electromechanical machines, does it quietly, requires minimal power, and fits in the palm of your hand.

All that—for a cost 99% lower than the old machines.

Now, let us go back to the days of the old electromechanical calculator. Imagine the President of a calculator company trying to reduce prices—through traditional cost cutting methods.

The President informs the factory manager that he does not like the way employees have been working, and he instructs him to set up and enforce—strict, tough work rules.

Need I say more? Even if the assembly lines had
been working at the old silent movies comedy speed, the
price of a calculator could never have been reduced by
99%.

> The calculator is a remarkable example of pro-
> ductivity improvement. If other sectors of in-
> dustry would have done as well—we could buy a
> means of transportation, not necessarily an au-
> tomobile as we know it now, for less than $100.

> And—we could let our world famous desert ag-
> ricultural experts show the Middle East coun-
> tries new uses for their oil fields.

COUNTERPRODUCTIVE
ASSUMPTIONS

Anyway, you should not think that I am trying to tell
you that Labor has nothing to do with productivity.

What I am trying to put across, is—that it is a grave
and misleading mistake to assume that Labor is the
major factor in productivity, and therefore—to assume
that productivity improvement is impossible, as long as
there is no change in the attitude of Labor, or for that
matter, in Government Regulations.

> In fact, my research indicates, so far, that La-
> bor and Government Regulations, are but 2 of 51

factors affecting productivity.

With such a figure, 51 factors, is it necessary to add that productivity is, indeed, a very complex subject, which should not be oversimplified, and, of course, could not be treated completely in one lecture.

However, what should (I hope) come out of this lecture, is that the first and basic requirement to achieve productivity improvement—is—to shake off any type of established, traditional, dogmatic, or political assumption about productivity.

R & D PURCHASING DEPARTMENT CASE HISTORY

One of my case history of productivity improvement is as far as possible removed from the "Labor" factor in productivity, since it involved the "Management" factor.

Specifically, productivity improvement was the result of a change in corporate management policy.

I worked on that project together with the Purchasing Manager for a large aerospace corporation.

The Purchasing Manager was trying to improve the productivity of his department, made up of some 250 employees.

I was trying to solve a frustrating productivity problem in the company's Research and Development Laboratories, an organization made up of several thousand engineers and scientists, plus supporting personnel. The Laboratories' problem was that important, critical projects—were delayed, or stalled—because of delays in the procurement of urgently needed parts, or other small items.

As you know, a very large organization does require many fiscal and management controls. The medium to carry out such controls is paperwork.

Everybody is aware that paperwork is usually slow, and costly to process. But how costly is often underestimated. At the time, this was the mid-fifties, the Purchasing Manager calculated that processing one purchase order meant a company cost of over $8!

In the Laboratories, while parts and materials needed for Research and Development projects were requested according to well planned schedules, it was not always possible to figure out, in advance, how many parts will be destroyed during testing, or even what will be needed during state-of-the-art research work.

One especially frustrating aspect of the problem was—that a part urgently needed may cost a few Dollars, or even a few Cents—much less than the cost of the paperwork to purchase it—and that further work had to be delayed—while waiting for a long administrative and management approval process to take place.

The answer to such a problem may seem obvious, but any of you who had experience with very large organizations will appreciate that it is not always that simple to provide a solution—when, as this was the case, it required changing an established corporate management policy.

The policy was that all purchasing actions had to be channelled through the Purchasing department. Under the changed policy, the Laboratories' departments were given petty cash funds, and allowed to make, directly, purchases up to an adequate Dollar amount.

Each department had a "property man" taking care of test equipment, materials and supplies. When more electronic components were urgently needed, the property man, following a simple departmental purchasing procedure, would drive to the nearest wholesale, or even retail store where the components were available.

Within a couple of hours, the purchase was delivered directly to the engineers who had made the request, thus avoiding work delays.

In other words, the changed management policy improved productivity in the Research and Development Laboratories.

In the Purchasing department, the change in management policy resulted in a significant decrease in the number of purchase orders issued, as well as in the paperwork, and other associated purchasing and handling tasks.

In other words, the changed management policy improved productivity in the Purchasing department.

I have given you two examples of productivity improvement.

Trying to characterize the two examples, we can say that the range of means, of processes are extreme.

The first example was the result of a series of design changes in calculators—made possible by the availability of new components—resulting from scientific research, engineering developments, and new manufacturing methods.

The calculator productivity improvement required large investments, took many years, and had sensational results, in the order of one hundred to one, an improvement ratio seldom achieved, although other examples could be found.

> The second example can be better described as a change in what I call an organization's "COMPREHENSIVE MANAGEMENT SYSTEM," as explained in my lecture titled "PRODUCTIVITY: NEW MANAGEMENT CONCEPTS."

Considering the size of the company, the few Dollars required to set up the petty cash funds, did not count.

Therefore, we can say that the productivity improvement required no cost, or investment.

While the results could not be valued in Dollars, if I could describe the effect—of administrative delays and frustrations—upon engineers and scientists struggling to advance the state of knowledge, while trying to beat contractual project deadlines, you will understand why, removing one administrative frustration was recognized, and appreciated as a significant productivity improvement.

> At the risk of repeating myself, the two examples had nothing to do with the most publicized and assumed causes of low productivity increase in the United States, such as:

> —Lack of investment capital for industry—lack of tax incentives to invest in research, in new facilities and equipment—attitude of Labor—and, of course, Government Regulations.

The same comments apply to many productivity problems I have solved, many improvement opportunities I have initiated, developed, and implemented.

This is why I am often tempted to climb on a soap box, and tell people to stop talking about the politics of productivity, and go down to the floor of their own shops, roll up their sleeves, and do something about productivity improvement.

I do know, from my own experience, that such an attitude will bring results.

PRODUCTIVITY   IMPROVEMENT PROCESS

Coming down from soap box enthusiasm, I must add that one should proceed carefully.

For example, one often difficult, but most important phase of productivity improvement—is the identification of problems—and sources of low productivity.

One aspect of the difficulty can be illustrated by one embarrassing situation I have encountered many times: An executive tells me about a problem in the management of his or her organization—then, proceeds to explain, and sometimes dictate the solution.

Productivity is a management function.

No management problem, no productivity problem can be solved without thorough analysis, or on the basis of hurried or superficial observations—or worse yet, on the basis of assumptions.

Identifying and analyzing sources and problems of low productivity—are but one phase of the productivity improvement process.

Other phases are:

To develop the methods, the means, the plans, to achieve productivity improvement, then, to carry out the implementation.

Notice that I do not advocate the use of any standard improvement method, or package: A standard package working in one productivity situation—does not indicate that it will meet the main, or specific requirements of another productivity situation.

Productivity improvement is—a management process.

Management cannot be standardized. If it could—managers would be replaced by a handbook, or by a computer.

WHAT MAKES PRODUCTIVITY IMPROVEMENT POSSIBLE?

Now, I would like to emphasize another major aspect—of what it takes to reach the "GOLD MINE" of higher productivity. What are the basic conditions, the basic requirements to achieve productivity improvement? There is—one overwhelming requirement—a positive answer to the following question:

> Is the very top management of the organization really willing, and ready to start a productivity improvement program?

I am not talking about making speeches, or announcing the formation of another committee—but rather about management's willingness, and readiness—to adopt a policy of productivity progress, and then, to implement that policy with sustained action.

For many years, the General Electric Company used a wonderful slogan in all its advertising:

> "At General Electric, progress   is our most important product."

This should be a universal slogan, because—one basic condition for any organization committed to productivity improvement, is to make progress—sustained progress, both a management policy, and—a management practice.

PROGRESSIVE/CONSERVATIVE
PRODUCTIVITY CONCEPTS

Speaking of "progress," two words in common usage are much misused, and misunderstood: The words are "PROGRESSIVE," and "CONSERVATIVE."

Of course, the misunderstanding comes from the political misuse of the words "conservative" and "progressive." It would be easy to amplify on this unfortunate semantic confusion, but we are here to talk about productivity, not about politics.

Let me illustrate the importance of the progressive and conservative concepts—as related to productivity, the words being taken in their basic meaning, usually found as the first definition in a dictionary.

Suppose—a manufacturing plant, managed under absolute conservative policies. Under such conditions, no change would ever be made to work methods, equipment, personnel policies, etc.   Under such "conservative" management policies, which do exist, the likelihood that productivity would go up—is rather slim.

What is highly probable, is that competitors with more "progressive" management policies will cause problems to the "conservative" plant, perhaps even drive it out of business.

OTHER REQUIREMENTS FOR
PRODUCTIVITY IMPROVEMENT

One other—basic requirement—to make productivity improvement possible, in absolutely any type of organization, is related to new ideas, and can be stated as follows:

> Within reasonable limits, and as applied to the widest range of organizational aspects—from general policy to the most detailed work method, management—must be absolutely open minded to new ideas, coming from any source.

I confess—that such a principle of productivity improvement came to me, as I recalled some productivity problems I have solved—in areas where I could not have any expertise, or experience, because no more than a few people in the world had ever gained such experience.   However, those were productivity problem situations—when management was desperate.

Many people have good—new ideas for productivity improvement. Many people have good ideas to prevent productivity problems. But—management must be receptive, management must be willing to listen.

THE OLD WORKER AND THE YOUNG BOSS

This reminds me of the little old shoemaker, who was the husband of my "concierge," or apartment building manager in Paris. He was working in a shoe factory. The owner retired, and his son took over the business.

Looking for ways to improve profits—he noticed that the cutters were disposing of a sizable part of the hides. The new owner ordered to stop that waste, and produce more shoes per hide.

The little old shoemaker was the only man in the factory with the courage, and the initiative, to walk into

the boss's office, and explain that some parts of a hide
are not good enough to make shoes.

Fortunately, the boss was in a good mood, and simply told the man to go back to his work station.

A few months later, the shoes started coming back.

Management must be willing to listen.

PRODUCTIVITY AND CHANGE

The next basic requirement for productivity improvement is the recognition, and acceptance that applicable
new ideas will necessitate changes, and that changes
require analysis, evaluation, planning, and—
implementation.

PRODUCTIVITY LAW
INTRODUCTION

Ladies and gentlemen, please forgive a few words of
philosophy. The history of human knowledge indicates—that it does take a long time to accept new facts,
later taken for granted, even when such facts are easy
to identify.

It would be presumptuous to make a parallel—with
the earth rotating around the sun, and a few others.
However, one important fact became obvious during

my studies of productivity, and led me to formulate a "PRODUCTIVITY LAW."

While my PRODUCTIVITY LAW is very simple, its introduction does require some very elementary arithmetic.

Simple implications of the basic productivity formula provide an explanation of the relationship between work and productivity—which is startling, because it is contrary to established, prevalent opinions.

The basic organization productivity formula states:

PRODUCTIVITY = OUTPUT / RESOURCES

(Productivity equals output divided by resources.)

"RESOURCES" are made up of many components: Labor, Equipment, Facilities, etc.

Let us consider the Labor component only, and let us call it "WORK." The productivity formula is then:

PRODUCTIVITY = OUTPUT / WORK

(Productivity equals output divided by work.)

Few people ever liked dealing with fractions in school. Anyway, that productivity formula, that simple fraction, tells us something very important.

Keeping in mind the following condition:

GIVEN, REASONABLE OUTPUT GOALS
ACHIEVED BY AN ORGANIZATION.

The organization productivity formula tells us:

(1) Productivity tends to go down, as people are working more.

For example, if a task is accomplished with 1,200 hours of work, productivity is lower than if it is completed with 1,000 hours of work.

(2) Therefore, and keeping in mind our given condition, productivity tends to go up, as people are working less.

(3) Ideal productivity conditions—are reached—when most people have little work to do.

This last statement may sound like a joke. However, it does apply exactly, to what I observed, many years ago, while visiting a Coca Cola bottling plant. What the typical worker was doing there, would have been described in the old days as "doing nothing:" Just sitting—in front of moving machinery, watching bottles go by.

The high productivity bottling plant example should not detract from what I have stated before: The general concepts of productivity—and productivity improvement, are not limited to automated processes, to assembly lines, and do apply to services, technical and managerial activities, where one can often find unsuspected, or little publicized productivity problems.

I have analyzed and solved productivity problems in many types of organization. Each case confirmed the simple productivity formula analysis I gave you.

Each and every time—I found people working harder and harder, while failing—increasingly, to reach their output goals. This led me to formulate a "PRODUCTIVITY LAW."

Listening to (or reading) the first of the three statements making up my PRODUCTIVITY LAW can be unsettling, because it is contrary to well established thinking, contrary to much cherished traditions.

Well, here we go . . .

BIALEK'S PRODUCTIVITY LAW

(1) Low productivity is—usually—associated with hard work. To amplify:

(2) Hard work—required—to achieve reasonable output goals—indicates low productivity.

(3) Hard work—not sufficient—to achieve reasonable output goals—indicates a productivity problem.

NOTE: My "law" is derived from the observation of low productivity and productivity problem situations. What is the most direct implication to avoid such situations? An old-fashioned management concept, still widely believed, was to make people work harder to achieve higher productivity. The old concept is wrong. It is worth repeating, and keeping in mind, that higher productivity is achieved through means of production requiring less hard work.

Now, in summary . . .

TO REACH AND EXPLOIT THE GOLD MINE OF PRODUCTIVITY

1. It is necessary to remember that productivity depends on all levels, all aspects of an organization: The assembly line as well as the executive offices, the tangible, such as—a machine, as well as the intangible, such as—a management system—a policy.
2. It is necessary to avoid making assumptions about productivity.
3. It is necessary to avoid the confusion—between—appearance of effective work, and real work results.
4. It is necessary to make and sustain a commitment to productivity improvement.
5. It is necessary to thoroughly analyze productivity problems, and productivity improvement opportunities.
6. It is necessary to develop the methods, means, and plans—to achieve productivity improvement, then—to carry out the implementation.
7. It is necessary to accept progress—to seek and make progress.
8. It is necessary to be receptive to new ideas, coming from any source, and applied to any aspect of the organization.
9. It is necessary to accept change. However, any proposed, or planned, or forced change must be analyzed for its effect on productivity.
10. It is necessary to make productivity improvement an integral part of the functions of an organization.

Thank you.

LECTURE 4

PRODUCTIVITY: RESOURCES AND RESOURCE FACTORS

SUMMARY: Productivity definitions, formulas, and index for the firm or organization level. Productivity system concept. Resources identification and types. Description of 51 productivity resource factors.

INTRODUCTION

Ladies and Gentlemen:

First, I would like to deal with one of the great stumbling blocks preventing productivity improvement action.

Keeping in mind that:

Productivity is a management responsibility.

Productivity is a management function.

With regard to the theory and practice of management, one question deserves great attention:

Is it always possible to quantify management?

Or, is it always possible to translate management plans, management actions, management evaluations, into precise, bottom line figures?

The answer is NO, and this answer, this fact is extremely important, because it applies to productivity, and more so to productivity improvement.

It may be frustrating not to be able to attach a reliable cost-effectiveness figure to every productivity improvement action. Well, not every environment, not every organizational situation is conducive to exclusive Dollars and Cents evaluation.

This fact, tells us that sound management dictates productivity improvement action, even if it is not possible to place a Dollar sign on the bottom line, and I will prove it with a number of examples, later.

The preceding statement does not imply that productivity can always be improved.

IS AN IMPROVEMENT "PROGRAM" NEEDED?

When I was studying management and organization, the typical model of work environment was "a shop."

I remember a good old professor—giving the example of a new shop, set up with a small number of competent workers, performing some not overly complex machining and assembly functions. Such a shop, the professor stated, has no need for engineers, or "efficiency experts." Within a short time, the workers will have figured out the best ways to handle the shop's production. At this point, engineering efforts to improve productivity would be a waste of time and money.

This was sound advice to young engineers who think—they can improve everything.

Later on, I found out that some—not necessarily young—engineers, managers, and consultants, sport the same "I can improve everything" attitude—with costly consequences for the organizations they are serving.

Productivity is no problem in a simple environment.

Productivity becomes an increasing problem as the work environment, the organization, becomes larger, or more complex.

In an extremely complex environment, productivity can even be very difficult to perceive. Therefore, productivity losses will tend to occur, without management being aware of it.

Hence, the necessity—for management—to look for existing or potential productivity losses, and to take corrective action.

PRODUCTIVITY DEFINITIONS FORMULAS

There are many aspects to productivity. One reason why productivity is difficult to evaluate, or even perceive, is because many of its aspects are "concepts," which we will try to elucidate later.

In the meantime, and starting with a relatively simple outlook, how can we define productivity?

Productivity is usually defined as a RATIO, a relation between "figures." Deciding what the "figures" in the ratio are, is the first difficulty. However, we assume that productivity increases when the value of the ratio increases, and vice-versa.

SIMPLE PRODUCTIVITY DEFINITION

One simple productivity definition is:

(1) PRODUCTIVITY = RESULTS / TIME

(Productivity equals results divided by time.)

Suppose one shop produces 100 widgets in an 8-hour day.

If production, in the same time, goes up to 110 widgets, the productivity ratio is up.

If 9 hours, instead of 8, are required to produce the 100 widgets, productivity is down.

Productivity formula (1) is simple, and does have applications, as we will see later. Unfortunately, it is also simplistic: It tells too little about the productivity situation.

PRODUCTIVITY IMPROVEMENT EXAMPLE: FARMING

One of the most ancient human work endeavor is—digging into the earth, into a field, with a plow, or other agricultural implement, for the purpose of growing food—farming.

Taking a quick look at the history, the evolution of that work endeavor, we start with a man pulling a plow.

The first step in increasing the early farmer's productivity was to use an ox, or a horse to pull the plow. Since a horse's pulling power is greater than man's, more field area could be plowed in one day, meaning increased results, increased productivity.

Let us skip certain civilizations, where the farmer's wife was pulling the plow—the wealth of a farmer being described by the number of wives he owned.

The next historical productivity leap came from the engine powered tractor pulling the plow, or other agricultural implement. The farmer, or farm worker, is driving the tractor. Of course, the farm worker can accomplish much more with a tractor than with an ox—or a horse.

Finally, we have the huge agricultural machine—still driven by one man, sitting in an air-conditioned cabin, listening to music, or to the latest commodity news, while accomplishing—in one day, several hundred times more than his ancestor, who was slaving in the hot sun.

In other words, the historical LABOR PRODUC-TIVITY of the farm worker went up several hundred times.

On that basis, we could say that the formula:

(1) PRODUCTIVITY = RESULTS / TIME

is a good definition, except that it tells nothing about how productivity improvement was achieved. Therefore, we have to introduce the economics of the farming situation.

When plowing was performed with an ox, probably fed from a field owned by the farmer, and fertilized by the ox (a very efficient arrangement), most of the cost of plowing was the salary paid the worker, assuming the farmer had employees.

Today, the investment in the huge machine piloted by the worker is enormous. The yearly cost of paying off and maintaining the machine is many times the salary and fringe benefits paid the worker.

Comparing the work combination, or unit, made up of the worker and the ox, against the work unit made up of the worker and the agricultural machine, we can draw some valuable conclusions.

First conclusion: The daily results of the machine combination is several hundred times that of the ox combination. Labor productivity is several hundred times higher.

Second important conclusion: The several hundred fold increase in labor productivity has nothing to do with the farm worker. The productivity increase is entirely due to the equipment.

Third conclusion: As stated in previous lectures, thinking about productivity in exclusive terms of "labor productivity" is obsolete.

Fourth conclusion: Since the formula

(1) PRODUCTIVITY = RESULTS / TIME

has no provisions to accommodate the cost of equipment, while it can be used for some productivity evaluations, it is not adequate for a comprehensive productivity definition.

The most common productivity definition is the formula

(2) PRODUCTIVITY = OUTPUT / INPUT

(Productivity equals output divided by input.)

This is the formula used by economists, both for theory, and for actual productivity measurements.

"OUTPUT" is the value of what the work unit, or firm, or nation, is producing. It can be wheat, automobiles, etc. At the national level, it can be the Gross National Product (GNP).

"INPUT" is the cost of the means of production, actually made up of several, or "aggregate" inputs.

For economic analysis, the simplest combination of INPUTS is LABOR and CAPITAL.

In our farm productivity improvement example, in

terms of economic analysis, the equipment would be defined as "capital."

At the "firm" level, INPUT will be made up of several appropriate cost components, such as Direct and Indirect Labor, Materials, Energy, adjusted costs of Facilities, Equipment, etc.

Note that I have used the professional economists' language, such as "firm," "aggregate," "equipment" defined as "capital." This makes it easier to understand an economist during a television interview.

BASIC 'PRODUCTIVITY' SYSTEM CONCEPT

While the word "INPUT," as previously defined, is standard in Economics, from a productivity management standpoint, there is one good reason not to use it: It is confusing.

Why confusing?

Because it is impossible to talk about the management of productivity—without talking about WORK PROCESSES.

It is impossible to talk about work processes without thinking in terms of SYSTEMS.

Finally, it is impossible to talk about SYSTEMS,

without using the word INPUT, which has a different meaning than "input" as defined for the economic analysis of productivity.

Example: An office, with clerical workers processing documents.

For a productivity analysis of that office, if we use formula (2) "productivity equals output divided by input," "input" means the cost of processing the documents.

Now, for a SYSTEMS analysis of that office, "INPUT" means the actual documents coming in for processing.

To clear up the semantic "INPUT" word confusion, we can look, first, at the BASIC SYSTEM CONCEPT of a work process, made up of "black boxes," as follows:

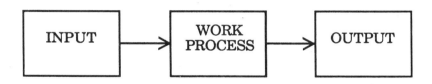

INPUT → WORK PROCESS → OUTPUT

Fig. 1 Basic system concept

For the productivity analysis of a SYSTEM, we need more black boxes, because the "WORK PROCESS" includes too many components, and productivity considerations, such as:

1. The WORK PROCESS is a mixture of tangible and intangible elements. For example, verifying and approving a document is an obvious action. A verbal instruction to consult with a supervisor if the document amount is over $1,000, is not obvious.

2. The WORK PROCESS is affected by many FACTORS. For example, a design change in the INPUT may require a change in the number of employees. Or, the hiring of inexperienced personnel may slow down the rate of OUTPUT, thus reducing productivity.

The basic 'productivity' system concept is better illustrated with two more "black boxes," as follows:

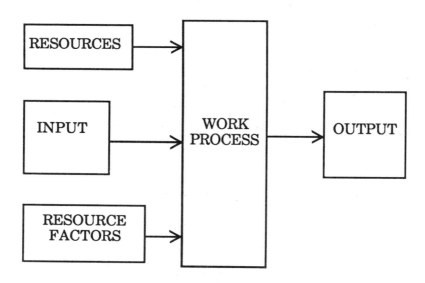

Fig. 2 Productivity system concept

In the preceding block diagram:

"RESOURCES" includes LABOR, plus all the means necessary to produce the OUTPUT.

"RESOURCE FACTORS" includes POLICY, plus many other factors to be described later.

"INPUT" affects both RESOURCES and RESOURCE FACTORS.

For productivity evaluation, the cost of INPUT must be added to the cost of all other RESOURCES required to complete the WORK PROCESS.

CONCEPTUAL PRODUCTIVITY FORMULA

Now that the "INPUT" confusion has been eliminated, we can formulate productivity as:

(3) PRODUCTIVITY = OUTPUT / RESOURCES

(Productivity equals output divided by resources.)

From the preceding 'productivity' system block diagram, and as stated in my lecture titled "PRODUCTIVITY: NEW MANAGEMENT CONCEPTS," comprehensive productivity evaluation requires expansion of above productivity formula (3) to:

(4)   PRODUCTIVITY = OUTPUT + OUTPUT
FACTORS / RESOURCES + RESOURCE FACTORS

(Productivity equals output plus output factors divided by resources plus resource factors.)

NOTE: Productivity formula (4) above is a conceptual
representation, absolutely necessary to understand the complexities of productivity and productivity improvement. It is not for the economic or accounting measurement of
productivity.

PRODUCTIVITY INDEX

Now, if it is necessary to develop and maintain a productivity index for an organization, a formula can be
used, indicating the percentage change of a ratio, between a base period and a measured period.

(5) PRODUCTIVITY INDEX = $\dfrac{\text{OMP/RMP}}{\text{OBP/RBP}}$ x 100

Whereby:
    OMP = OUTPUT— MEASURED PERIOD
    RMP = RESOURCES — MEASURED PERIOD
    OBP = OUTPUT—BASED PERIOD
    RBP = RESOURCES — BASE PERIOD

The values of OUTPUT and RESOURCES are in
Dollars.

How the OUTPUT and RESOURCE values should be adjusted, and aggregated—is a question of cost accounting.

The ultimate result is to measure changes in productivity. Therefore, some accounting simplifications may have no significant effect on the practical value of the productivity index.

For example, if you are interested in nothing less than a 5% change in the index, a 1% change in one of the index elements can be ignored.

PRODUCTIVITY DEFINITIONS RESOURCES AND RESOURCE FACTORS

RESOURCE IDENTIFICATION TEST

In trying to define, or identify a resource, or resource factor, the first question is:

"Is it a resource or resource factor?"

The answer is "YES"— if:

"A MODIFICATION OF THE RE-SOURCE, OR RESOURCE FACTOR, AF-FECTS PRODUCTIVITY."

TYPES OF RESOURCES AND RESOURCE FACTORS

In most organizations, most work situations, we can find

3 TYPES OF RESOURCES AND RESOURCE FACTORS

1. TANGIBLE or OBVIOUS
2. INTANGIBLE or NOT OBVIOUS
3. INTANGIBLE or LESS OBVIOUS

NOTE: In studying productivity, in evaluating a productivity situation, it is possible to argue endlessly about which is either a resource or a resource factor, and, if intangible, if it belongs in above defined Type 2 or Type 3.

The classification is not important. What is important, is the identification, and then the understanding of "what" has been identified, how it affects productivity, and how it should be modified to improve productivity.

Let us consider a resources identification example.

A RESTAURANT KITCHEN

You are not performing a comprehensive survey or analysis.

You are walking through a restaurant kitchen, and you see a man working. What he is doing indicates that he is a Chef. This is a fairly simple work situation. What are some of its resources and resource factors?

1. TANGIBLE OR OBVIOUS

— The Chef. This is the LABOR resource.
— Stoves, refrigerators, pots and pans. This is EQUIPMENT.
— Meats, vegetables, other ingredients. This is MATERIALS.

2. INTANGIBLE OR NOT OBVIOUS

— The Chef's EXPERIENCE: Not obvious, because it could not be evaluated without observation of his work. The same applies for his TRAINING: Did he work for several good restaurants? Did he serve an apprenticeship under a great Chef?
— Other factor not obvious: An instruction from the restaurant owner, as to, for example, how much butter the Chef can use. This is a MANAGEMENT POLICY.

3. INTANGIBLE OR LESS OBVIOUS

— A salary, or work conditions dispute between the Chef and management.
— A running feud between the Chef and some waiters.

We could probably find many more possible resources and resource factors in this "simple" work situation.

IMPORTANT PRODUCTIVITY MANAGEMENT CONSIDERATIONS

The last example of INTANGIBLE OR LESS OBVI-OUS FACTOR, "feud between the Chef and waiters," is the most important to consider, for the management of productivity improvement.

Here are a few reasons:

1. Undue stress will affect the Chef's work, therefore the quality of the food served by the restaurant. Lower quality will, eventually, affect the restaurant's volume of business.

2. Since the volume of business is a restaurant "output," its reduction means a change in productivity. This is the test of a productivity resource factor.

3. It is impossible to measure—how undue stress in the restaurant kitchen affects productivity: Slower business can also be due to weather, competition, etc.

4. Management action to solve the undue stress situation will improve productivity.

5. No reliable measurement of the productivity improvement action can be done: An improvement in the restaurant's business can be due to external factors, such as an influx of tourists. External factors can also reduce business volume, thus compensating for a real productivity improvement.

In addition to the five remarks made so far, the most important points of this example, which apply to most work situations, and were stated in my lecture titled "PRODUCTIVITY: NEW   MANAGEMENT   CONCEPT," are as follows:

6. Measurement is not the necessary first step of productivity improvement.

7. Difficulty, or impossibility to measure productivity should not, must not prevent productivity improvement action.

PRODUCTIVITY   RESOURCES   AND RESOURCE   FACTORS   DESCRIPTION

NOTE 1   The resource listing sequence, as will be stated, does not imply a hierarchy. The relative importance of a resource, or resource factor, is specific to each organization, and will change with time, circumstances.

NOTE 2   The listing 'classification' can be argued, because many factors can be both tangible and intangible. However, as stated earlier, this would not be a constructive exercise. In fact, "discussing classification" is a classic method—to reduce work productivity.

TANGIBLE OR OBVIOUS RESOURCES AND RESOURCE FACTORS

1. MANPOWER / LABOR

This basic resource is affected by many factors, to be considered later.

2. FACILITIES

Where a work process is performed.

3. EQUIPMENT

Includes machinery, furniture, computers, etc. In the old days, management paid little attention to the relationship between FACILITIES, EQUIPMENT, and productivity. Much progress is still needed in this area.

4. MATERIALS / SUPPLIES

Requires no explanation, except that a change in materials can change the time and cost required to complete a production process, therefore affect productivity.

5. POWER / ENERGY

This is an example of a productivity factor which can be of insignificant value in some cases, such a small organization housed in rented offices, and very important in cases where energy is a major cost, such as a "smokestack" industrial plant.

6. SERVICES

Includes 'external' Accounting, Legal, Computer, Advertising, Consultant, and other services.
It can also be an 'internal' staff set up as a service to the organization.

7. CAPITAL

Industrial history, and economics, show that CAPITAL is a major productivity improvement factor. Providing, of course, proper planning and utilization of the capital investment.

8. TIME

This is a good example of useless discussion of classification, since we are listing a "tangible" resource.
The dictionary definition of "tangible" is: "Capable of being touched."
Except in science fiction, nobody ever "touched" time. Yet, the resource identification test: "Does its modification, or change, affect productivity?" applies directly to TIME, since a given work process completed in 'reduced' time means an 'increase' in productivity.
Furthermore, TIME is the basic element of any PLANNING process. Therefore, it is a tangible productivity resource factor.

INTANGIBLE OR NOT OBVIOUS RESOURCES AND RESOURCE FACTORS

9. DESIGN

While the DESIGN of a manufactured object, an administrative document, is 'apparently' obvious, it is not obvious that a modified design can often reduce manufacturing or processing time, thus increasing productivity.

10. METHODS

" 'Tain't what you do, it's the way you that do it." This popular song, written by Sy Oliver in 1939, is a good description of one of the most important productivity factors, regardless of the type of work process.

Introducing the concept of METHODS in the work place, was probably the greatest contribution to productivity made by the pioneers of scientific management.

11. PROCEDURES

While METHODS usually refers to one task, or one work process within one organizational unit, PROCEDURES often refers to a work process moving through several organizational units.

The word PROCEDURES is also used instead of METHODS in most administrative organizations.

12. ORGANIZATION

Refers to the unit of people and means where the work process is performed, as well as to the overall structure and type of a group of work units.

13. POLICIES

Includes management, personnel, and any other type of POLICY used in the organization.

Example: Delegation of authority.

14. COMMUNICATIONS

Can be called a by-product of the factors ORGANIZA-TION, POLICIES, and PROCEDURES.
In this context, bad COMMUNICATIONS is, of course, a negative productivity factor, and must be corrected for productivity improvement.

15. SYSTEMS

Assuming that SYSTEMS means "computer systems" is a conceptual mistake. Many times, I have seen the costly consequences of that mistake.
The computer, what it has been programmed to do, combines with all work processes affected by the computer inputs and outputs to form a SYSTEM.
In other words, what is called the "computer system" should be looked at as one element of a larger, and total SYSTEM.

16. PLANNING

Includes work and machine loading or scheduling, formulation of resource requirements, output objectives, short range and long range considerations, etc.
Periodically, new names are coined to define a specific area of PLANNING, such as "capacity management," "needs assessment," "time management," etc. Well—like for "productivity improvement," the program name is not important—as long as it is done.
Lack of PLANNING is, without doubt, a negative productivity factor, because it prevents an orderly production process.
Excessive planning is also a negative productivity factor, because it makes undue time demands on management and staff personnel, delays decision making, and the execution of work processes.

One important aspect of PLANNING is "disaster planning." Already widely used in Data Processing functions, it should be extended to all functions of an organization.

It is important to remember that the productivity value of any type of PLANNING, depends on periodic updating.

17. VOLUME

In general, "higher volume" results in increased productivity. However, such a principle should not be taken for granted, because every step increase in VOLUME can create new problems, having a negative effect on productivity.

18. SIZE

At one time, the concept of "bigger is better" was accepted by the public, and widely used in advertising campaigns. Then, the "small is beautiful" proponents proved that a small organization is more efficient than a large one.

The fact is, there is no direct relationship between SIZE and productivity. A large organization can afford more capital equipment increasing productivity. On the other hand, a large organization has more requirements, and is more difficult to manage than a small one. Therefore, the productivity gain from increased capital resources can be lost without attention to all other productivity factors.

INTANGIBLE OR LESS OBVIOUS RESOURCES AND RESOURCE FACTORS

19. ABSENTEEISM

This frustrating negative factor, affecting the MAN-POWER / LABOR resource—becomes obvious in its extreme case: A strike, bringing organization productivity down to zero.
The ABSENTEEISM problem is usually related to other resource factors, to be considered later.

20. PERSONNEL TURNOVER

Since this is a negative productivity factor, it is always amazing to me—how often the management of organizations affected by this problem—do little to correct it.
PERSONNEL TURNOVER is also, usually related to other intangible factors, such as POLICIES.

21/22. SKILLS / EDUCATION

There are still some occupations where SKILLS is not a major LABOR productivity factor. However, the percentage of workers in such occupations has been going down, and the trend indicates further reductions.
While skills results from EDUCATION and EXPERIENCE, EDUCATION, not directly job-related, can also be a positive productivity factor.

23. JOB DESIGN

This is a comprehensive productivity factor, related to other resource factors, such as METHODS, ORGANIZATION, etc.

24. TECHNOLOGY

Progress in TECHNOLOGY is one of the most important productivity improvement factors. The factor is not limited to manufacturing, since most organizations use the product of technology. Example: A new diagnosis device, improving the productivity of medical services.

25/26. RESEARCH / ANALYSIS

This is a comprehensive productivity factor, usually positive, leading to other productivity improvement factors.

Without RESEARCH (from basic research, to applied Research and Development,) there would be no new MATERIALS, or DESIGNS, or EQUIPMENTS, or METHODS.

I can also state, from repeated observations, that implementing new—POLICIES, ORGANIZATION, PROCEDURES, SYSTEMS—without adequate RESEARCH and ANALYSIS, is a sure way to reduce productivity.

There is one RESEARCH activity directly related to productivity improvement work: To find out what was done in the past, in similar situations—through internal and external interviews, literature search, state of the art surveys, etc.

Failure to engage in such "historical" RESEARCH results, at best, in loss of time, and, at worse, in enormous and costly blunders.

27. GOVERNMENT

All politics aside, GOVERNMENT has both positive and negative productivity effects. For example, requiring an organization to have a safety program is positive, while requiring excessive paperwork is negative.

In any case, the GOVERNMENT factor, including REGULATION, cannot be ignored.

28. EXTERNAL FACTORS

Many factors—EXTERNAL to the organization, can affect productivity.

Examples: A change in an industry connected with the organization, a change in currency value, a change in the price of a basic commodity (such as oil), a major transportation strike, unusual weather conditions, etc.

All such changes affect the resources costs, therefore productivity.

29. WORK ENVIRONMENT

This is a 'comprehensive' productivity factor, reflecting the effect of several other factors.

From a tangible standpoint, it refers to the quality of FACILITIES, such as work space (or crowding), noise level, etc.

The intangibles are psychological factors, such as the effect of MANAGEMENT STYLE and POLICIES.

The productivity value of the WORK ENVIRON-MENT factor was demonstrated by the classic 'Hawthorne Study', which took place from 1924 to 1939, and is discussed in many books on the psychology of management and employee relations.

30. TRAINING

The fast changing nature of the economy requires periodic upgrading of employee SKILLS and EDUCATION.

Very successful corporations, providing generous-training and education, on company time, have found it to be a good investment for productivity improvement.

31. EXPERIENCE

Assuming an employee's learning period is over, the productivity value—of more EXPERIENCE, is related to the complexity of the work processes taking place in the organization, and to the possible lack of EXPERIENCE of other employees.

Many times, I have seen one mistake made by a new manager: Not to take advantage of the experience accumulated by an old time employee. Such an employee may not offer radical productivity improvement ideas, but remembers all the changes, and mistakes made in the past. Drawing on the experience of old time employees during the planning of productivity improvement programs, can save time, money—and red faces.

32. MANAGEMENT TALENT

This productivity factor does not refer to managers. It refers to an employee's ability to manage tasks and assignments on an individual, nonsupervised basis.

33. TEAMWORK

A most valuable, positive, 'synergistic' productivity effect results from cooperative work between organizational units or levels, between Management and Labor, and, of course, between workers.

34. ENGINEERING EFFICIENCY

Waste is a negative productivity factor. An organization reducing waste improves its productivity: This is ENGINEERING EFFICIENCY.

Of course, the factor has also "mechanical" meanings: An engine wasting less fuel, a building wasting less heat, etc.

35. SUPPORT

The availability to one organizational unit, of help, or services, or resources, from another organizational unit.
With regard to SUPPORT, large corporations have usually a productivity advantage over small companies.

36. CONTROLS

Should be a positive factor. CONTROLS are a negative productivity factor when lacking, or excessive.

37. MANAGEMENT STYLE

MANAGEMENT POLICIES reflect MANAGEMENT STYLE, and are, sometimes, spelled out in writing.
There are many aspects to that factor, reflected in a large body of literature.
The main STYLES are "autocratic" and "democratic," although the usual classification includes also "bureaucratic" and "laissez-faire." However, my observations are that bureaucratic and laissez-faire styles are not exclusive, but usually subcharacteristics of one of the two main styles.
With regard to the "autocratic" management style, I have no doubt that it is a negative productivity factor.

38/39. LEADERSHIP / EXECUTIVE TALENT

In most types of organization, good leadership is a positive productivity factor.
Again, a large body of literature defines the many aspects of LEADERSHIP and EXECUTIVE TALENT.
However, in some forms of organization, 'lack' of leadership is also a positive productivity factor.

Example: An autonomous group, where the workers make and implement management decisions. One famous illustration of this example is known as the "Volvo experiment," whereby the traditional assembly line was replaced by groups of workers responsible for one element of the automobile assembly. The workers of the group make, on their own, most management decisions.

40. ORGANIZATION CULTURE

Generally, ORGANIZATION CULTURE is not a direct productivity factor, since it is reflected by MANAGEMENT STYLE and POLICIES. However, it is important to pay close attention to ORGANIZATION CULTURE during productivity improvement work: It can explain the background of productivity problems, it can indicate if an improvement method is liable to succeed or fail.

On a direct productivity factor basis, the literature on international marketing is abundant with horror stories of corporate resources going to waste while trying to establish a market in foreign countries. The reason is that the way of doing business in that foreign country may be different from the way it is done in the United States. Learning the local business CULTURE and practices should be the first step of an international marketing effort.

The same principle is valid within the United States. Different marketing principles have to be used in different parts of the country, in rural or metropolitan areas, in dealing with a big corporation as opposed to a small business, with a government agency as opposed to a private business.

41. COMPREHENSIVE MANAGEMENT SYSTEM

This important productivity factor was introduced in my lecture "PRODUCTIVITY: NEW MANAGEMENT CONCEPTS." The components of this "SYSTEM" include the ORGANIZATION, its structure, its POLICIES, its PROCEDURES, and the SPECIFIC SYSTEMS used to carry out the work process.

It is a 'system' because all its components interact with each other to establish the productivity framework of the organization.

42. KNOW-HOW

The value of KNOW-HOW, acquired by a person or an organization, is often misunderstood, generally underestimated.

KNOW-HOW cannot be precisely defined. It is a combination of practical knowledge, practical experience, skills, mental record of successes and failures, of fruitful ideas as well as mistakes, etc.

KNOW-HOW cannot be found in books, or manuals, or blueprints: Only in people.

For the productivity of an organization, KNOW-HOW is one of the most valuable assets.

43. JOB SATISFACTION

In recent years, more and more attention has been given to JOB SATISFACTION, for example through "job redesign." However, many workers are still complaining about job 'dissatisfaction,' a negative productivity factor.

Proof that job dissatisfaction is a widespread problem can be found in Social Security statistics: 2/3 of the workers applying for retirement are under 65.

44. MOTIVATION

Of course, an important employee productivity factor, at all levels of an organization.
MOTIVATION is closely related to the next factor . . .

45. MORALE

I have seen many managements paying no attention to employee morale: A costly mistake, because MORALE does affect productivity.

In extreme cases of low morale, I have seen productivity going down to zero, because output was down to zero, as employees had good reasons to wonder about the future of their jobs.

To improve MORALE, I have seen managements doing "nice" things for their employees: The lasting effect on productivity was zero, sometimes negative.

The causes of MORALE problems must be identified, in order to plan corrective action. It is not an easy task.

46. LOYALTY

Lack of employee loyalty is difficult to detect, except in extreme cases—such as embezzlement.

Less extreme cases are reflected by excessive employee turnover, absenteeism, reduced output quality, and low productivity.

On the other hand, excessive loyalty required by some executives, in the form of absolute approval, and conformity, is also a negative productivity factor, since it dampens the generation of innovative ideas and actions.

Of course, identifying and correcting the causes of LOYALTY problems will have a positive effect on productivity.

47. "SECRET ATTITUDE"

This employee productivity factor, usually negative, is difficult to define: It is almost the same as LOYAL-TY, but not quite.

For example, an employee decides to only "appear" working for two hours each day. Or, abstains to communicate constructive ideas.

There is often a relationship between the MANAGE-MENT STYLE factor, and the "SECRET ATTITUDE" factor, which makes the problem difficult to correct, because changing the MANAGEMENT STYLE of an organization is difficult.

Companies affected by a widespread "SECRET ATTI-TUDE" productivity problem have a tendency to be absorbed by larger corporations, or go out of business.

48. ALIENATION

A comprehensive productivity factor, one step worse than the negative aspects of the "SECRET ATTITUDE" factor. It is reflected by some of the factors already described, such as ABSENTEEISM, TURNOVER, lack of MOTIVATION and of LOYALTY. However, ALIENA-TION can also be expressed through worse actions, such as systematic waste, sabotage, pilferage, and even violence.

ALIENATION in the work place is but one aspect of the more general problem, and has, of course, been studied by sociologists.

Correcting organization ALIENATION problems is within the scope of another comprehensive productivity factor: The COMPREHENSIVE MANAGEMENT SYSTEM.

49. NORM SETTING

This often negative productivity factor is similar to the "SECRET ATTITUDE" factor, but extended to the group, or organization level.

For example, all workers in a shop have a tacit agreement as to their rate of production. Such an agreement can even be formalized by an union contract.

On the other hand, management groups also set norms for their attitude towards workers, which may or may not be written in company policy manuals.

One famous worker norm breaking example took place in the Soviet Union, in the late twenties. Stakanov, a coal miner, proved to his fellow-workers that one man can produce several times the daily amount recognized normal, by workers and management.

Stakanov became a "hero" of the Soviet Union, went around the nation lecturing, and establishing the "Stakanovite" movement.

"Stakanovism" was worker productivity improvement through a mixture of patriotic dedication, improved work methods, athletic and mental self-training for increased performance. It was an early form of what is now called "super-achievement."

50. CORRUPTION

This negative productivity factor can be present in government, as well as in private business and non-profit organizations.

For example, CORRUPTION can increase the cost of an organization's resources, and decrease the quality of the organization's output.

Establishing adequate purchasing procedures will

prevent, or solve many—but not all—aspects of the CORRUPTION productivity problem.

51. INNOVATION

This is, also, a comprehensive productivity factor, since it is the result of RESEARCH, of new METHODS, new PROCEDURES, new SYSTEMS. It is also the result of MANAGEMENT STYLE, and of POLICIES oriented towards accepting change, seeking new ideas.

It is extremely important to remember that significant productivity improvement is impossible—without INNOVATION.

Next to the MANAGEMENT factors, INNOVATION is, by far, the most important factor for productivity improvement.

RESOURCES AND RESOURCE FACTORS — SUMMARY

The following table summarizes the resources and resource factors described.

TABLE III PRODUCTIVITY RESOURCES AND RESOURCE FACTORS

TANGIBLE OR OBVIOUS
1. Manpower / Labor
2. Facilities
3. Equipment
4. Materials / Supplies
5. Power / Energy
6. Services
7. Capital
8. Time

INTANGIBLE OR NOT OBVIOUS
9. Design
10. Methods
11. Procedures
12. Organization
13. Policies
14. Communications
15. Systems
16. Planning
17. Volume
18. Size

INTANGIBLE OR LESS OBVIOUS
19. Absenteeism
20. Personnel turnover
21/22. Skills / Education
23. Job design
24. Technology
25/26. Research /Analysis
27. Government
28. External factors
29. Work environment
30. Training
31. Experience
32. Management talent
33. Teamwork
34. Engineering efficiency
35. Support
36. Controls
37. Management style
38/39. Leadership / Executive talent
40. Organization culture
41. "Comprehensive management system"
42. Know-how
43. Job satisfaction
44. Motivation
45. Morale
46. Loyalty
47. "Secret attitude"
48. Alienation
49. Norm setting
50. Corruption
51. Innovation

TABLE III—NOTES

1. The relative importance of each factor is specific to a given situation at a given time. Example: Sometimes a task is done well without leadership. Sometimes task leadership is the most important success factor.
2. Specialized factors specific to one organization or one type of activity should be added to the list.

RESOURCES AND RESOURCE FACTORS—CONCLUSION

We have identified 51 factors affecting the productivity of an organization. Improving any one factor is likely to improve the productivity of an organization. However, many factors interact with each other, and several factors may require change to obtain improvement.

For example, an improved computer system may have no positive, or even a negative effect on productivity, unless some POLICIES and PROCEDURES related to the new system are changed, or unless a related productivity problem in any organization affected by the new system has been corrected.

Also, it is always necessary to make sure that a positive change to one factor—will not have a negative effect on another factor. If it does, a benefit analysis will indicate if the proposed improvement change is still a good idea.

It is worth repeating that we have identified 51 productivity factors associated with the resources of an organization. Many organizations have additional specialized factors. The sheer number should be an abundant source of thought for any person interested in the management of productivity improvement.

Thank you.

LECTURE 5

PRODUCTIVITY: OUTPUTS AND OUTPUT FACTORS

SUMMARY:
Outputs identification and types. Description of 29 productivity output factors. Productivity improvement activity. The measurement question. Productivity improvement management situations. Productivity problems identification.

INTRODUCTION

Ladies and Gentlemen:

The previous lecture was devoted to the RESOURCE aspects of productivity. We did not exhaust the subject, and we will look at some important related problems in another lecture.

I have explained why I am using the word "resource" instead of the economics term "input," to avoid any confusion, while looking at a work process as a "system."

However, there is no possible confusion between system and economics productivity concepts, by using the word "OUTPUT."

The problem is—how to identify the outputs, because, from the standpoint of productivity, an organization has many OUTPUTS and OUTPUT FACTORS.

OUTPUT IDENTIFICATION TEST

The OUTPUT and OUTPUT FACTORS identification test principle, is the same as for resources and resource factors identification:

"A MODIFICATION OF THE OUTPUT OR OUTPUT FACTOR AFFECTS PRODUCTIVITY."

Another OUTPUT identification, which may appear simplistic, is:

"A MEANINGFUL DESCRIPTION."

Such an output identification is in line with modern marketing theory, which requires a company to ask: "What is our business?"

For productivity analysis, the question translates to: "What is our OUTPUT?" Past a few obvious items, the answer is not easy.

OUTPUT IDENTIFICATION EXAMPLES

Let us look at a simple OUTPUT productivity example:

A CHOCOLATE CHIP COOKIES SHOP

The shop bakes and sells one type of cookies only. How many OUTPUTS can we identify—for a given time period?

1. NUMBER of cookies sold.
2. WEIGHT of cookies sold.
3. DOLLAR VALUE of cookies sold.
4. REJECT WEIGHT, or DOLLAR VALUE—Can be broken cookies.
5. PROFIT.
6. WASTE / GARBAGE.
7. QUALITY.
8. POLLUTION—Most people like the smell of baking. Some may not.
9. COMMUNITY SERVICE—The owner gives day-old cookies to free-meal institutions, creates a summer job for a high-school student.
10. GOOD WILL—An intangible output factor, which does have a Dollar value when a business is sold.

This was a quick look at the cookies shop. It indicates that, for productivity analysis, there is more to OUTPUT than a Dollar figure.

Now, for a more complex OUTPUT productivity example, let us consider:

A PURCHASING DEPARTMENT

The department is part of a large organization. In addition to purchasing functions, the department is responsible for material and supplies stores, printing shops, mail service, and the office copy machines. For a given time period, what are the OUTPUTS?

1. NUMBER of Purchase Orders issued.
2. DOLLAR AMOUNT of Purchase Orders issued.
3. NUMBER of Purchase Requests processed— perhaps more significant than the previous outputs.

   From a "system" standpoint, a Purchase Request is an INPUT to the department. From a productivity standpoint, the 'processed' Request is an OUTPUT, with a complex value: 'More' Requests processed, without increased department RESOURCES, means 'increased' productivity. On the other hand, if the organization can function with 'less' Requests, 'less' department RESOURCES will be required, and this too means 'increased' productivity.

4. TIMELINESS—Are materials and supplies

available on the date requested?
5. ABILITY TO DEAL WITH EMERGENCIES.
6. ABILITY TO MANAGE OTHER DEPARTMENT SERVICES—Stores, printing shops, etc.
7. COST REDUCTION ABILITY—To find lower priced materials and supplies. To maintain a low level of inventory, without delays in supply.
8. "SATISFACTORY SERVICE"—This important output factor is difficult to evaluate. For example, some requestors may not give enough time to make "SATISFACTORY SERVICE" possible.

Several of the purchasing department output factors could be consolidated under the "QUALITY" factor, except that productivity analysis, or evaluation, requires more specific descriptions. However, QUALITY, for most organizations, should be evaluated as an important output productivity factor.

For the two examples given, 'more' output factors could probably be found. The purpose was to show what happens, when we try to identify an organization's outputs and output factors.

OUTPUT AND OUTPUT FACTORS CATEGORIES

Producing a comprehensive listing, as was attempted for RESOURCES, would not be possible, because each organization has its own "meaningful" OUTPUTS.

We can, however, attempt to identify some of the most often encountered outputs and output factors, always related to a given time period.

The 'productivity' meaning will be improved, by dividing the OUTPUT descriptions in two categories:

(1) PRIMARY / DIRECT

The most obvious, and sometimes easy to measure OUTPUT.

(2) SECONDARY / INDIRECT

Less obvious, sometimes a by-product of the PRIMARY / DIRECT outputs, usually difficult—or impossible to measure.

OUTPUTS AND OUTPUT FACTORS DESCRIPTION

NOTE. What was stated for the RESOURCE description listing applies for the OUTPUT listing also: The sequence does not imply a hierarchy, and the categorization is open to discussion.

PRIMARY / DIRECT OUTPUTS AND OUTPUT FACTORS

1. DOLLAR AMOUNT

Not necessarily a positive output factor. For example, if increased sales is achieved through reduction in PROFIT.

2. VOLUME / QUANTITY / NUMBER OF UNITS

Also, not necessarily a positive factor. For example, if increased VOLUME results in decreased QUALITY.

3. NUMBER OF SERVICE ACTIONS / CALLS

Same meaning as VOLUME, for service organizations.

4. SERVICE—PRIMARY OUTPUT

Less specific than the previous outputs. Refers to whatever a service organization is supposed to produce. For example: Design improvement, training, health care, etc.

5. REJECTS

This negative output can be expressed in Dollars, or in quantity.

6. MAINTENANCE

It could be argued that this is a "resource." However, MAINTENANCE is the valuable result of work, of a program.

For example, a manufacturing organization divides its resources to produce both, 'salable goods,' and 'maintenance' of its production facilities.

"Internally" produced maintenance can be looked at as an important output, "fed back" to the organization as a resource.

"Externally" purchased maintenance is strictly a resource. In both cases, it is an important productivity factor.

7. REPORTS

The primary, and sometimes only valuable output of some organizations. For example, the output of an economics research group.

Reports are also a secondary output. For example, "sales reports."

As a secondary output, excessive reports production is a negative productivity factor.

SECONDARY / INDIRECT OUTPUTS AND OUTPUT FACTORS

8. RESEARCH

An output less specific than REPORTS, and not limited to technical or scientific organizations.

Example: Marketing research. It can be the main output of an organization, or the output of a working group internal to the organization.

9. ADVICE

Also the output of either an external, or an internal organization, such as—a staff function.

10. TROUBLE

An obviously 'negative' productivity factor, with many, and more specific meanings, such as: "Machine down time."
TROUBLE is an output factor within the "feedback concept," because it affects the organization's resources.

11. ABSENCE OF TROUBLE

Reverse of the previous output factor. For example: "Number of manufacturing days without more than 5 minutes of machine down time."
When medical organizations become more productivity conscious, they may advertise, as one "output," the number, or percentage of clients—who did not take one day of sick leave during the past year.

12. SAFETY

One type of TROUBLE (negative factor), or ABSENCE OF TROUBLE (positive factor), important enough to be identified, and accounted for as one output.
SAFETY is also a "feedback concept" output factor, because it affects the organization's resources.
It can also be a more 'direct' output factor, for example the safety provided by a store to its customers, or by a transit system to its riders.

13. PROFIT

Depends, and is related to, other factors, such as RE-JECTS.

Of course, the positive output factor PROFIT, turns negative—if it is a LOSS.

14. QUALITY

Can be treated as both a positive or negative productivity factor, depending if we look at the percentage of output "good" or "bad."

In some cases, QUALITY can be measured by counting REJECTS, and through statistical methods—found in the Quality Control literature.

In other cases, it is a "subjective" evaluation, such as the quality of food preparation, and of other work processes resulting in a "service."

15. AVAILABILITY

Regardless if the output of an organization is a product, materials, supplies, or a service—"is that output available as agreed, or when needed?"

16. TIMELINESS

Are services performed, products delivered, according to agreed upon schedules?

17. RELIABILITY

A different way to describe some aspects of the previous output factors: QUALITY, AVAILABILITY, and TIMELINESS.

While the word "reliability" usually refers to a product, such as a machine, a piece of equipment, it is also the ability of an organization—to meet its planned objectives and commitments, without requirements for external supervision, or for follow-up actions.

18. FLEXIBILITY

The ability of an organization to respond to change—in planned schedules, in procedures, specifications, etc.

19. CUSTOMER ORIENTATION

Specific to the retail business, but applicable to any "customer" situation. It is a combination of several of the output factors described so far, and a major, positive productivity factor.

20. INTERNAL REQUIREMENTS

An output additional to the basic results of a work process. Example: Periodic reports to management.

21. EXTERNAL REQUIREMENTS

An output factor imposed by an agency external to the organization where the work process is taking place. Examples: A sales quota. An affirmative action program.

22. WASTE

No work activity, no work process is possible without the production of WASTE. Of course, the highest the percentage of waste in the output, the lowest the productivity.

Long before the word "productivity" was used in management circles, industrial and business managements implemented "cost improvement programs." One standard cost improvement method is the systematic reduction of WASTE. For example, a manufactured part is stamped out of sheet metal. After stamping, scrap metal is left over. This is WASTE. Changing the design of the part may allow the stamping of more parts per square foot of metal. The cost of each part is thus reduced, because the stamping shop's output includes a smaller percentage of WASTE. Cost improvement through waste reduction is applicable to most work processes. It results in improved organization productivity.

23. POLLUTION

POLLUTION is but one type of WASTE, but important enough to be identified as a specific output.

It is unfortunate that POLLUTION became associated with the politics of "Government Regulation," because the reduction of POLLUTION, or WASTE, engineered properly, increases efficiency, and productivity. For example, the reason why dirt particles coming out from a smokestack go up, is because they are pushed by heat. That heat is a waste of fuel, one resource used in the plant below the smokestack.

I have read success stories of industrial plants installing systems, which, at the same time, trap dirt, and recycle the heat previously lost. The savings in fuel pay for the anti-pollution system in a few years, and the plant is left with reduced production cost, meaning—improved productivity.

24. ENERGY CONSERVATION

A relatively new, but important secondary output, of concern to many organizations.

Energy conserved—means reduced cost of resources,

therefore, increased productivity.

25. COMMUNITY SERVICE

Most large corporations assign a percentage of their financial, and personnel resources to that output. Regardless of motives, it is now a widely accepted business practice.

26. GOOD WILL

An intangible output factor, with a definitive Dollar value. For example, an organization maintains high quality standards, which become known, and quoted in the trade. Or, a business maintains given levels of sales, profit, customer satisfaction. It all adds up to GOOD WILL, and is taken into account when the business is valued for sale.

27. SERVICE—SECONDARY OUTPUT

A comprehensive output factor, including several factors already described, such as QUALITY, AVAILABILITY, etc.

As a 'secondary / indirect' output, SERVICE refers to what an organization does for its customers, or clients, or other organizations served, first by strict compliance to contractual requirements, but mostly above and beyond customer expectations.

In the book "In Search of Excellence, Lessons from America's Best Run Companies," authors Thomas J. Peters and Robert H. Waterman give numerous examples of leading corporations where one top management policy is an almost obsessive attention to SERVICE to their customers. While the 'primary output' of such companies ranges from computers to potato chips, SERVICE is treated as the major output factor contributing to the company's success.

28. "MICRO / MACRO" OUTPUT VALUE

This is a productivity concept described in an earlier lecture under "Relative productivity evaluation."

The MICRO output of one small organization, contributes to the MACRO output of a larger organization. The productivity of the small organization may be high. However, the value of the small organization's output to the productivity of the larger organization is a different story: It can range from high to low.

For example, the success story of a new chief executive turning around a faltering corporation, may include the discovery of a staff group, producing fine work—of little or no use to the corporation. The productivity of the staff group can be high. If the output of the group is of no value to the corporation, the productivity of the group, from a corporate standpoint, is zero.

29. "BINARY OUTPUT" VALUE

In this computer age, it is appropriate to use the "binary" concept, whereby one item of information can have only two values: 1 or 0. "1" means that the item of information is there, and "0" that it is not there. In a computer, the information item is, basically, an electronic pulse.

Applying such a concept to measure, or evaluate, output productivity, may seem a little harsh. However, it is useful in the exercise of realistic management.

Now, "realistic" does not mean "dictatorship." It implies the management ability to identify potential problems, and to work out preventive solutions.

The BINARY OUTPUT productivity concept is—that the output of a work process can have only the two values "1" and "0".

Output "0" means that the work process is not "fully" completed, as planned. Output "1" means that the work process is "fully" completed.

The meaning of "fully" must be well understood by all parties involved with, or concerned by, the work process under evaluation.

The concept can apply to a project "task," as follows:

TASK STATUS	OUTPUT VALUE
NOT COMPLETED	0
COMPLETED	1

Fig. 3 Binary output value, applied to task status

Example: A computer system can be operational only after a number of programs have been written and tested. All programs are completely finished, except one. It makes no difference if work on the last program is 90% completed, or 98%. As long as it is not 100% completed, the computer system cannot be used.

In connection with the BINARY OUTPUT VALUE concept, it should be remembered that the productivity of a nonroutine task—is not "linear" in time. For example, my own experience in managing projects indicates, that if it took 9 weeks to achieve 90% completion, one more week will not, necessarily, achieve 100%.

The BINARY OUTPUT VALUE concept is important for the management of such projects, where the completion of one task is required to start another one.

It is also important for management planning decisions. For example, how long a commitment (which may include a contract, or a lease), should be made to a current system, or a current work process, until the new system or work process is really ready to go?

OUTPUTS AND OUTPUT FACTORS — SUMMARY

The following table summarizes the outputs and output factors described.

TABLE IV   PRODUCTIVITY OUTPUTS AND OUTPUT FACTORS

PRIMARY / DIRECT

1. Dollar amount
2. Volume / Quantity / Number of units
3. Number of service actions / Calls
4. Service—Primary output
5. Rejects
6. Maintenance
7. Reports

SECONDARY / INDIRECT

8. Research
9. Advice
10. Trouble
11. Absence of trouble
12. Safety
13. Profit
14. Quality
15. Availability
16. Timeliness
17. Reliability
18. Flexibility
19. Customer orientation
20. Internal requirements
21. External requirements
22. Waste
23. Pollution
24. Energy conservation
25. Community service
26. Good will
27. Service—Secondary output
28. "Micro/Macro" output value
29. "Binary output" value

TABLE IV—NOTE

Specialized factors specific to one organization or one type of activity should be added to the list.

OUTPUTS AND OUTPUT FACTORS CONCLUSION

We have reviewed 29 outputs and output factors.

One problem for economists, and anyone concerned with productivity, is the difficulty to measure outputs, even when such outputs have a Dollar value.

We have seen that for many outputs and output factors, it is very difficult to assign a Dollar value, if not impossible.

We have limited our review of outputs and output factors to the firm, or organization.

At the national level, measurements are more difficult yet, and we will not get into that problem.

Spending time on precise measurements is not necessarily a productive activity.

For example, one of the many books on cost reduction I have read, relates the study of a typing pool, with an analysis of typing work listing several hundred items! Such as: "Inserting 1 original and 2 copies—0.393 minute."

Output evaluation, adapted to the real needs of productivity improvement management, is usually enough, if not more meaningful.

We will look further into productivity measurement, but first, I would like to describe an example . . .

THE STOREKEEPER'S RE-ORDER SYSTEM

Once, I was evaluating a stores inventory system, including inventory of forms.

The system reports indicated re-order points for given inventory levels. In studying the reports, some data did not seem right. So, I went to see the storekeeper in charge of forms, and asked him how he used the reports.

He pointed at a file cabinet in a remote corner: "When I receive a report, I stack it up there, and leave it until next month's report comes in, then it goes in the round file."

"So, how do you know when a form has reached the re-order point?"

The storekeeper took me to the forms shelving area. Pointing at one stack, he said: "This is a heavy usage form. When the stack is down to here (about two feet high), it is time to re-order." Moving on, "this is a low usage form; down to here (a few inches), I re-order."

The storekeeper evaluated forms usage in feet and inches. This may offend some proponents of scientific management, but the storekeeper's system worked.

In scientific management, and its extension, systems analysis, measuring or expressing inputs, outputs, and other factors, with three decimal places, may give a false sense of doing the right thing.

What is right, is to use the most appropriate evaluation—for each management situation.

It can be a 99.99% accurate count.

Or it can be a comment, such as "better," or "worse."

PRODUCTIVITY IMPROVEMENT ACTIVITY

PRODUCTIVITY MEASUREMENT

In my lecture "PRODUCTIVITY: NEW MANAGEMENT CONCEPTS," I reported one academic opinion, and one actual example of the possible catastrophic results of productivity measurement.

Yet, there are case histories—of measurements improving productivity.

The study of many case histories indicates a range of possible measurement outcomes.

One or more of the following possibilities can result from a measurement program.

PRODUCTIVITY MEASUREMENT OUTCOME POSSIBILITIES

1. IMMEDIATELY BENEFICIAL

The program produces improvement in the organization—without anything else being done to improve productivity. Employees are motivated to improve their performance.

2. EASY AND VALUABLE

The measurements provide a good base, and first step, for a productivity improvement program.

3. DIFFICULT

Measurement is a problem.

4. SUBJECT TO OPINION

Objective evaluation of measurement results can draw different conclusions.

5. LOSS OF TIME

Nothing is gained from the measurement program.

6. DETRACTS FROM REAL IMPROVEMENT EFFORTS

Too much emphasis is placed on measurements, and not enough on actual improvement efforts.

7. PREVENTS IMPROVEMENT FOR A LONG TIME

Employees of the organization "measured" are turned off against the productivity improvement people, and will refuse cooperation for future improvement attempts.

8. REDUCES PRODUCTIVITY

Employees resent the measurements, and engage in systematic slow down.

9. REDUCES OUTPUT QUALITY

Stronger worker resentment, translated into systematic lowering of quality, and in extreme cases, sabotage.

10. DAMAGES LABOR RELATIONS

Needs no explanation.

11. TRIGGERS A STRIKE

The ultimate measurements damage and loss, for Labor and Management. In the previously mentioned lecture, I gave the example of the 1978 Safeway strike, triggered by a measurement program at the distribution centers.

So much for the possible outcomes of a productivity measurement program.

The activities and literature related to measurement have inspired one of my "productivity laws," which I will give you at the end of this lecture series.

Of course, a productivity improvement program should have an objective, even if that objective is not associated with a specific measure, such as a Dollar figure. Example: "Reduce the percentage of customer complaints."

Also, in lieu of measurements, there is no harm in using existing data, produced by accounting, planning, and other operational systems.

MEASUREMENT OUTCOME SUMMARY

The following table summarizes possible outcomes of productivity measurement.

TABLE V PRODUCTIVITY MEASUREMENT OUTCOME POSSIBILITIES

1. Immediately beneficial
2. Easy and valuable
3. Difficult
4. Subject to opinion
5. Loss of time
6. Detracts from real improvement efforts
7. Prevents improvement for a long time
8. Reduces productivity
9. Reduces output quality
10. Damages labor relations
11. Triggers a strike

Now, let us talk about productivity improvement, and the many aspects of productivity improvement management.

PRODUCTIVITY   IMPROVEMENT   SITUATIONS

People trying to improve productivity are faced with many situations.

To a large extent, the potential results of productivity improvement work depend—on the circumstances prevailing when the work is started.

Some often encountered productivity improvement situations can be described as follows.

1. LOW PRODUCTIVITY, MANAGEMENT DOES NOT CARE

In this case, it takes "astute salesmanship" to propose productivity improvement.

Even if management is doubtful of the outcome, the improvement program can be started, providing— reasonable assurance that management will support it.

However, it must be recognized that productivity improvement work, under such conditions, is still a gamble.

2. LOW PRODUCTIVITY—IS—A TEMPORARY MANAGEMENT POLICY

Low productivity can be obvious to an outside observer. However, making or expressing hasty conclusions can be a mistake.

There are circumstances, when management is aware of low productivity, but accepts it on a temporary basis.

For example, pending a planned reorganization study. Or, while retaining excess capacity in equipment and trained personnel, because a future increase in work load is either planned, or anticipated.

3. MANAGEMENT CONCERNED ABOUT PRODUCTIVITY

This does not mean that productivity in the organization is low. Management may seek improvement to increase profit, or to gain a greater share of the market, or to counteract the effect of inflation, or to solve a budget problem.

Under such conditions, and providing management is willing to follow up its concern with action, an improvement program has a good chance to succeed.

4. A PRODUCTIVITY PROBLEM IS EVIDENT TO MANAGEMENT

Improvement work will be supported by management.

The potential difficulty is—if management wants to impose its solution to the productivity problem, without allowing adequate time and efforts to ascertain what the real problem is, and to develop appropriate solutions.

5. A PRODUCTIVITY PROBLEM IS DANGEROUS TO MANAGEMENT

The ideal productivity improvement situation exists—when management is desperate.

For example, a project is stalled, and several improvement efforts have failed. At this point, management will be willing to try solutions rejected under any other circumstances. Such an "ideal" situation should not minimize the challenge to solve the problem. Also, it must be recognized that careful analysis may reveal a problem situation—which cannot be solved. The solution is then, to develop a plan to minimize the overall effects of the productivity problem.

IMPROVEMENT SITUATIONS—SUMMARY

The following table summarizes the improvement situations described. Of course, not all situations fit into a neatly defined category.

TABLE VI PRODUCTIVITY IMPROVEMENT
SITUATIONS

1. Low productivity, management does not care
2. Low productivity—is—a temporary management policy
3. Management concerned about productivity
4. Productivity problem evident to management
5. Productivity problem dangerous to management

PRODUCTIVITY PROBLEMS

PRODUCTIVITY PROBLEMS MANIFESTATION

Low productivity is not necessarily evident. For example, as explained for the "micro/macro output value" concept, a group of employees, in their small organization, may be working efficiently, while their work output is totally useless to the larger organization.

Also, a temporary and anticipated low productivity situation should be differentiated from a permanent one. For example, during a switch to a new system, a new work process, or new equipment, a normal lowering of productivity can be expected, until all the "bugs" are worked out, and the learning process is completed.

Some obvious signs—indicating the existence of a real productivity problem, are:

1. Output quantity, or volume, is lower than planned, or "reasonably" expected.

2. Number of work in process errors, or rejects, has increased.

3. Quality has decreased.

4. Number of returns, or complaints, has increased.

5. A project completion schedule lags the planned schedule.

6. Overtime, or more personnel, are needed to meet planned schedules.

   NOTE: Overtime required to compensate for an unforeseen event is not a productivity problem sign. Examples: Accidental equipment destruction, unexpected customer demand.

7. A backlog has accumulated. The problem is worse, if the backlog is increasing.

   NOTE: A backlog productivity problem should not be confused with a situation where a firm tries to maintain a "portfolio" of customer orders, thus avoiding frequent changes in production requirements.

8. Verification of BIALEK'S FIRST PRODUCTIVITY LAW: Employees are working hard, and can-

not achieve reasonable output goals.

Again, a differentiation should be made between temporary hard work required, for example, to meet an emergency, and hard work required all the time. The latter is evidence of a productivity problem.

PRODUCTIVITY PROBLEMS MANIFESTATION—SUMMARY

TABLE VII SOME PRODUCTIVITY PROBLEM SIGNS

1. Output lower than planned
2. Increasing rejects, work process errors
3. Decreasing quality
4. Increasing returns, complaints
5. Lagging completion schedule
6. Chronic overtime
7. Backlog, increasing backlog
8. Hard work does not achieve output goals

NOTE

While all the "signs" listed above pertain to problems I analyzed, this cannot be a comprehensive list. Management should learn to recognize early productivity problem signs developing in their organization. Many productivity problems tend to be recurrent.

PRODUCTIVITY PROBLEMS IDENTIFICATION

A productivity problem is a management problem. A management problem must be identified, because the "obvious" cause often turns out to be secondary to the real cause of the problem.

> Many times, I went through the embarrassing experience—of a manager describing a problem, then proceeding to state what must be done to solve it.

Much work can be required between productivity problem perception—and solution, starting with identification.

Productivity problems can be identified by a number of "techniques." Because management is not a mechanical process, we can say that the technique, or combination of techniques to use, are the ones which "appear" to be the most appropriate to identify the problem. While we will go into the productivity improvement "work" later, at this point, it is worth stating that the management of productivity improvement requires much experience, and judgment.

Now, trying to develop a "standardized" problem identification procedure would be counterproductive, because even if it was possible, it would result in much wasted efforts, in such cases where most of the identification procedure would bear no significant results.

EXPERIENCE

The first way to identify a productivity problem is not really a "technique": It is called "experience."

Such experience is not, necessarily, directly related

to a given number of years, and its utilization does not require formal methods.

For example, some experienced physicians claim, that by the time a patient walks in and sits down in front of their desk, they have a good idea of the patient's condition.

Some persons—experienced in solving management and productivity problems, can take a slow walk through a work area, and by the time the walk is over, have a good idea of what is going on in the organization.

It is probable—that the "experienced" professional, while observing, is performing a great amount of analysis, in a very short time. However, how such analysis is done, is not quite known yet.

Besides "experience," the other analysis techniques to draw upon are well documented in the literature.

The listing given next does not imply a sequence.

To repeat, it is better to use what is most "appropriate" for the situation.

> Because the choice of one analysis technique is based on a preliminary judgment, if the results are not conclusive, the work performed is not necessarily a loss of time: It can help in narrowing down the problem.

PRODUCTIVITY PROBLEMS IDENTIFICATION TECHNIQUES

1. EXPERIENCE

Already explained.

2. MANAGEMENT ANALYSIS

Study of the management processes in the organization.

3. POLICY ANALYSIS

Includes the analysis of official, unofficial, and sometimes nonexistent policies guiding the organization.

4. ORGANIZATION ANALYSIS

The study of groups or various units making up the organization, and of their structure. Also, the study of formal and informal channels of work communications.

5. SYSTEMS ANALYSIS

"Systems" is meant in its widest context, not limited to computer systems, and ranges from the general "COMPREHENSIVE MANAGEMENT SYSTEM" concept, to specific work or operational systems.

6. PLANNING ANALYSIS

The study of the organization's planning practices and methods.

Once, my finding that one problem, with an organization, is caused by a lack of planning, was challenged by a supervisor, who took me to a small slate hanging on a wall. The activities planned for the day were listed on the slate.

The lesson I learned, was that any analysis work must be clearly defined, and explained to the people affected by it.

7. METHODS ANALYSIS
8. PROCEDURES ANALYSIS
9. PROCESS ANALYSIS

The words METHODS, PROCEDURES, and PROCESS, really have the same meaning, but are used in different work settings. The meaning is—"how" the work, the task, is accomplished.

Analyzing work methods was the first innovation of the pioneers of scientific management. In a broader context, it is still one of the most fruitful basis for productivity improvement.

10. FORMS ANALYSIS

Analyzing forms, reports and other documents should not be done without systems and procedures analysis. A "forms" problem is often the tip of the iceberg.

11. VALUE ANALYSIS

Can be defined as "the identification of unnecessary cost."

One can say "of course, to improve productivity, we eliminate waste, unnecessary tasks and costs." Except that waste is not necessarily obvious, and thorough analysis is required.

12. DESIGN ANALYSIS

Applies to industrial, as well as to administrative processes. Example: A form design.

13. EQUIPMENT ANALYSIS

Analysis of the means of production.

One of my productivity improvement cases—was with a manufacturer of television components, using a home made piece of test equipment to check compliance with specifications. When customers had miscalculated their purchasing requirements, they returned a shipment, claiming the components did not meet specifications.

The manufacturer's engineers did not agree, but management could not be sure who was right, and had to issue a credit.

I recommended the purchase of a moderately priced test equipment unit, recognized world wide as a laboratory standard.

The test equipment purchase was well publicized by management and sales people. From that time on, the company had no more problems with customers requesting credits for low quality shipments.

14. COST ANALYSIS

Can be a by-product of VALUE ANALYSIS, or done by itself, with a cost accounting orientation.

15. PARETO CONCEPT ANALYSIS

Usually applied to Quality Control, it can be used for any finding resulting in data.

The principle is—that examination of the data shows that the total value of a few of the data elements amounts to approximately 80% of the grand total value of all data elements. Concentrating on what caused the reading of the few top data elements only, will bear the most productive results.

For example, 10 working groups are contributing to a project. Examination of progress reports indicates that 3 of the 10 working groups are responsible for most task completion delays. The obvious answer is to concentrate productivity improvement efforts on the 3 problem groups.

16. WORK SAMPLING

Specially useful for activities far removed from assembly lines, or continuous production situations, such as maintenance work, services, professional and management functions.

Work sampling is based on random observations, and has been written up in many books and industrial magazines.

17. COMPETITIVE, OR COMPARISON ANALYSIS

Whenever possible, such analysis consists of comparing the same organization at different time periods, or the organization under study with another, similar organization.

Such an exercise should be practiced with care—because it can be disturbing to management.

For example, it is not unusual to look at an organization of busy and hard working people—and discover that five years earlier, the same organization was fulfilling the same functions, with half as many employees.

18. EMPLOYEE SKILL EVALUATION

Can indicate training needs, or personnel structure changes—required to optimize the organization.

19. EMPLOYEE MORALE AND ATTITUDE EVALUATION

This is a delicate task, to be conducted by experienced specialists only.

20. WORK ENVIRONMENT EVALUATION

Applies to both tangible and intangible environment. This important topic will be examined later.

21. GROUP DISCUSSION

This problem identification method should be employed with extreme care.

There is a large body of literature on "group dynamics" related to solving problems, setting policy, stimulating creativity.

For example, a simple expression of each group participant's opinion, may uncover an unexpected aspect of the problem, or reveal a surprising attitude within a large segment of personnel.

One well publicized type of group discussion, "brainstorming," can suggest radically new solutions to a problem.

On the other hand, what behavioral scientists call "groupthink," is the result of a lack of analytical and evaluation work by the group, leading to the wrong decision. One tragic historical example—is the U.S. foreign policy group decision leading to the Bay of Pigs invasion.

22. SURVEY ANALYSIS

There is no formal definition of "SURVEY" in relation to improvement work.

The SURVEY implies a relatively short duration project.

It consists mostly of open, not hidden observation of work activities, with questions asked to a cross section of employees. The questions to ask depend on the problem under study, the observations made, previous answers, and other input.

The SURVEY may be sufficient to identify productivity problems, or can indicate that a more specific identification methods should be used.

The SURVEY can also be a preliminary action to evaluate a productivity problem. For example, SURVEY conclusions can be:

"A thorough ORGANIZATION ANALYSIS should be performed."

"Because of such circumstances, the productivity problem should be evaluated again in six months from now." Etc.

PROBLEM IDENTIFICATION TECHNIQUES — SUMMARY

The techniques described are summarized in the following table.

TABLE VIII PRODUCTIVITY PROBLEMS IDENTIFICATION TECHNIQUES

1. Experience
2. Management analysis
3. Policy analysis
4. Organization analysis
5. Systems analysis
6. Planning analysis
7. Methods analysis
8. Procedures analysis
9. Process analysis
10. Forms analysis
11. Value analysis
12. Design analysis
13. Equipment analysis
14. Cost analysis
15. Pareto concept analysis
16. Work sampling
17. Competitive, or comparison analysis
18. Employee skill evaluation
19. Employee morale and attitude evaluation
20. Work environment evaluation
21. Group discussion

NOTES

1. "Experience" is the best guide in selecting the one or several techniques required to identify a productivity problem. While it can be tempting to set up a selection table, the multiplicity of productivity problem situations would make such a guide misleading. If one analysis started—appears wrong, the work done should be recorded, because the results may save time during a future

productivity improvement effort.

2. Some activities may require the development of specialized problem identification or evaluation techniques.

3. The results of identification work provide a basis for the productivity problem solution. A minor problem, clearly identified, may not warrant further work.

CONCLUSION

We have taken a productivity improvement management look at the outputs of an organization, and at work measurements. We have described some of the general management attitudes encountered while attacking a productivity problem, and we have reviewed 22 productivity problems identification techniques. While one or several of the techniques listed should cover most situations, some productivity problems may require specialized identification methods.

To repeat, there is no effective—"standard" method for productivity improvement, or any of the work leading to productivity improvement.

The best method—is the one tailored to the specific problem situation.

Once the productivity problem is identified, we are ready for "productivity improvement action."

This is the topic for the next lecture.

Thank you.

LECTURE 6

PRODUCTIVITY: IMPROVEMENT PROGRAM ACTION

SUMMARY:
Productivity problems: Solution development and analysis. Improvement program development. Productivity improvement work and organization. Recurrent sources of low productivity.

INTRODUCTION

Ladies and Gentlemen:

During the previous lecture, we reviewed the methods of productivity problem identification.

Productivity improvement, like any other work endeavor, should be performed on the basis of specific goals—spelled out, even if such goals are obvious. So, let us look at:

THE BASIC PRODUCTIVITY IMPROVEMENT GOALS

A productivity improvement MATRIX can be set up on the basis of a simple productivity formula, using a Dollar value to define the output and resource costs.

For the formula

$$\text{PRODUCTIVITY} = \text{OUTPUT VALUE} / \text{RESOURCE COSTS}$$

The improvement MATRIX will look as follows:

PRODUCTIVITY	DOLLAR OUTPUT VALUE	DOLLAR RESOURCE COSTS
IMPROVED	INCREASED	SAME
IMPROVED	SAME	REDUCED

Fig. 4 **Productivity improvement matrix**

The MATRIX illustrates "end results."
To achieve such results, it is necessary to
engage in many tasks of . . .

PRODUCTIVITY IMPROVEMENT ACTION

We start at a point where management recognizes—
and accepts, that there is a productivity problem. The
problem must be described and analyzed. In other
words, a clear statement should indicate what it does to
the organization. Example: "The reject rate has doubled."

In previous lectures, we have reviewed a number of
"techniques" to narrow down, identify a productivity
problem.

Once a productivity problem has been identified, the
principle of the solution is usually obvious, which does
not mean simple.

If the solution is not obvious, it must be developed.

TASK PLANNING SEQUENCE

How to proceed with the phases of productivity work,
can be illustrated by the following sequence chart.

[1]	PRODUCTIVITY PROBLEM RECOGNIZED / ACCEPTED BY MANAGEMENT	[1]
[2]	PROBLEM DESCRIPTION	[2]
[3]	PROBLEM ANALYSIS	[3]
[4]	PROBLEM IDENTIFICATION	[4]
[5.1]	SOLUTION OBVIOUS SOLUTION NOT OBVIOUS SOLUTION DEVELOPMENT	[5.2] [5.3]
[6]	SOLUTION ANALYSIS	[6]
[7]	PROGRAM DEVELOPMENT	[7]
[8]	SELLING / APPROVAL / ACCEPTANCE	[8]
[9]	IMPLEMENTATION FEEDBACK ACTION [ ]	[9]
[10]	FOLLOW-UP	[10]

Fig. 5 Productivity tasks planning sequence

NOTES

1. The left or right sequence is followed, depending if the solution is "obvious" or not.

2. Why the FEEDBACK ACTION sequence is not indicated will be explained later.

PRODUCTIVITY PROBLEM
SOLUTION DEVELOPMENT

One should be careful with "obvious" solutions to productivity problems.

Example: Clerks are observed "working hard" to prepare a document. Revising and improving the document is the "obvious" solution. However, the bad (or obsolete) document design can be but the tip of the iceberg. While the document has to be improved anyway, much other work may be required to really solve the productivity problem.

Solving a productivity problem requires creativity.

When creativity is a little sluggish, a solution development checklist can help to trigger a good idea.

It is very important—to keep in mind—that a checklist cannot apply to all situations.

BASIC SOLUTION STARTING IDEAS

Looking at a work process, a design, or whatever appears to cause the problem, we ask questions, such as indicated in table below.

TABLE IX   SOLVING A PRODUCTIVITY PROBLEM—SOME BASIC STARTING IDEAS

1. Is there an alternative?
2. Is it an output?
3. Why is it done?
4. Who needs it?
5. Can it be optimized?
6. Can it be eliminated?
7. Can it be changed?
8. Can it be substituted?
9. Can it be combined?
10. Can it be improved?
11. Can it be simplified?
12. Can it be created?

PRODUCTIVITY PROBLEM
SOLUTION ANALYSIS

After the solution to a productivity problem has been selected and developed, it must be analyzed. Often, the analysis indicates a trade-off, whereby a productivity gain in one area results in a productivity loss in another area. The trade-off must then be evaluated.

One form of trade-off analysis is the popular "cost-benefit" analysis, which is often the basis for government decisions.

It should be realized that trade-off analysis, or cost-benefit analysis, does not work—when dealing with intangibles, or with facts not readily associated with a Dollar sign.

Looking at the next checklist for solution analysis, it must be emphasized, again, that effective productivity improvement work must be specific to the problem situation, and that a generalized checklist may not include some required specialized solutions.

BASIC ANALYSIS STARTING IDEAS

Looking at, keeping in mind the solution developed, we ask questions, such as indicated on the following table.

TABLE X ANALYZING A PRODUCTIVITY PROBLEM SOLUTION SOME BASIC STARTING IDEAS

1. What are the benefits of the solution?
2. What are the costs?
3. What are the effects on resources? Example: Requirement changes for manpower, or for equipment.
4. What are the effects on the work process inputs?
5. What are the effects on outputs?
6. What are the effects on systems?
7. What are the effects on other, same level organizations?
8. What are the effects on higher, and lower organization levels?
9. What are the effects on outside organizations? Examples: Vendors, services, contractual agencies.
10. What is the solution implementation schedule?
11. What are the effects on other planning?

PRODUCTIVITY IMPROVEMENT PROGRAM DEVELOPMENT

There is no general rule as to how to develop a productivity improvement program, since it depends completely on the problem solution, the environment, the circumstances.

The TASKS PLANNING SEQUENCE chart, described previously, can be a program guideline.

However, one fact is sure, an improvement program must be developed with a clear statement of objectives, tasks description, manpower and other requirements, detailed plans and schedules.

Depending on circumstances, the contents of the improvement program statement can range—from a "book," to a one-page short statement.

PROGRAM NAME

As mentioned in my lecture "PRODUCTIVITY: NEW MANAGEMENT CONCEPTS," it is often better not to mention the word "productivity," because many people still associate the word, or the idea, with old-fashioned "efficiency expert" stories.

If, for example, a productivity problem exists in the processing of documents, there is nothing wrong with "Document Processing Improvement Program."

The program name can refer to a specific resource, or output, or problem, such as "Reject Rate Improvement," or "Zero Reject Rate Program."

One of the oldest name for productivity improvement is "Work Simplification Program." It refers to a systematic evaluation—and improvement, of design, methods, procedures, and other resources and resource factors.

PROGRAM ACCEPTANCE AND IMPLEMENTATION

As indicated in the Tasks Planning Sequence Chart, the productivity problem solution has been developed, analyzed, and an improvement program has been developed.

Next, the program must be "sold" to management.

After management approval, it must—again, be sold to the employees affected. This is not difficult—if the employees affected have participated in the improvement work done so far.

> The principle of employee participation increases the success chances of a productivity improvement program by as much as several hundred percent.

On the other hand, improvement program development without employee participation has a high probability of reduced effectiveness—if not failure.

It should also be remembered that the implementation of a productivity improvement program always implies change, and that it can affect a number of resources.

For example, a change in one method, or procedure, may also require changes in job designs, equipment, organization, etc.

IMPROVEMENT PROGRAM FEEDBACK ACTION

Not indicated in the productivity improvement Tasks Planning Sequence Chart, is "where" the feedback action starts, and where it goes. The reason is, that any time during an improvement program, new discoveries, new internal or external factors, may require a program change, or new analysis, new development, etc.

There is an important implication here, and we will talk about it, as we look at productivity improvement work.

PRODUCTIVITY IMPROVEMENT WORK

THE WORKER

What was just said about "feedback action," indicates that people doing productivity improvement work must, first of all, be flexible, be willing to modify their plans.

And, if somebody has a better idea, the productive attitude is to use it, while, of course, giving full credit to the author of the suggestion or idea.

> The ability to perform good productivity improvement work is not limited to one specific educational or professional background.

> However, it is not an entry level activity, and I am always amazed by the fact of freshly graduated MBA's going directly into consulting work.

Management experience helps. A person with hands on responsibility for the output of an organization acquires a practical sense of realities, required for the implementation of productivity improvement.

Because of the range of disciplines which might be involved, the productivity improvement worker must be at ease with theoretical thinking, as well as with shirt sleeves action.

Rather than going into all the details of what makes a good productivity worker, it is better to emphasize one characteristic only, because it is by far the most important:

> This is CREATIVITY, the ability to see new and different ways. And also, the courage to propose something radically different, to take a risk, and to admit a mistake.

GENERAL CONSIDERATIONS FOR PRODUCTIVITY IMPROVEMENT WORK

As stated in my previous lecture, the ideal environment for productivity improvement work exists, when management is desperate to solve a problem. Under such conditions, full cooperation is available, not only from management, but also from employees, who may worry about the consequences of a serious productivity problem going unsolved.

Now, assuming that a productivity improvement program is starting; such a program can take place in a wide range of situations. For effective program management, the following considerations should be kept in mind.

1. PRODUCTIVITY IMPROVEMENT IS NOT A WORK OUTPUT

Every organization has to produce "something." With the exception of a productivity improvement function, "improvement" is not the organization's output.

2. PRODUCTIVITY IMPROVEMENT IS NOT A PRIMARY JOB DUTY

Employees are expected to do something else. Time spent on productivity improvement activities will reduce the time spent on regular job activities.

3. IMPROVED PRODUCTIVITY MAY INDICATE POOR PAST JOB PERFORMANCE

The long range success of productivity improvement work will be compromised, if the proof of poor past organizational performance is emphasized, and used to reduce the job rating of some employees.

4. PRODUCTIVITY IMPROVEMENT MAY CHALLENGE MANAGEMENT COMPETENCE

Circumstances will reduce, in time, the potential productivity of any organization. For example, the availability of a new method, makes an older method obsolete.

Much more important than dwelling on what happened in the past, is top management's real willingness to improve productivity, in the present.

5. PRODUCTIVITY IMPROVEMENT IS A THREAT TO ESTABLISHED PATTERNS

Productivity improvement always implies change.

A large percentage of people feel comfortable in what they are doing—even if it is wrong. Acceptance of change can be a problem—much reduced if, as already stated, employees participate in the formulation of productivity improvement.

6. PRODUCTIVITY IMPROVEMENT IS A THREAT TO JOB SECURITY

Except when improvement is aimed at solving a serious problem, the reality must be faced, that there are only two types of improvement: (1) More output with the same resources, and (2) same output with less resources.

"Less" resources has a high probability of meaning less personnel. Personnel reduction as a result of productivity improvement is a potential problem which must be faced before improvement work takes place. Solving the problem increases the chances of productivity improvement success. Ignoring the problem, not having a constructive plan, can reduce, or compromise the success of a productivity improvement program.

IMPROVEMENT WORK CONSIDERATIONS SUMMARY

How productivity improvement work is approached means the difference between success and failure. The main points to consider are summarized below, and apply to the organization where the improvement work is to be done.

TABLE XI IMPROVEMENT WORK CONSIDERATIONS

1. Not a work output
2. Not a primary job duty
3. May indicate poor past performance
4. May challenge management competence
5. Threat to established patterns
6. Threat to job security

NOTE

Each organization or situation may require additional items, or persons to be considered in planning the work.

FUNCTIONAL SCOPE OF PRODUCTIVITY IMPROVEMENT WORK

1. ONGOING ACTIVITY

Ideally, productivity improvement should be an ongoing function within each organization. Such a function will be examined later.

2. ONE-TIME PROJECT

A one-time effort is usually aimed at solving a well defined, often urgent productivity problem.

Outside of productivity problem solving, "one-time" and productivity improvement are incompatible concepts, because the permanent need to improve productivity is a normal occurrence in any organization.

The reason for conceptual incompatibility, already stated before, are inescapable internal and external changes, new requirements, new problems, and—progress.

The well managed organization responds to change through productivity improvement.

3. PERIODIC ACTIVITY

Between "ongoing" and "one-time" activities, a PERIODIC concept can be applied, whereby, for example once a year, a productivity review takes place. The review can then be followed by a limited program, to correct uncovered deficiencies, and to try some new improvement ideas.

PRODUCTIVITY IMPROVEMENT WORK: ORGANIZATION

Regardless of scope, one-time, ongoing, or periodic activity, productivity improvement can be organized either as:

1. A COMPANY WIDE PROGRAM

There is no full-time personnel implementing productivity improvement, although in a large organization, there may be some full-time leadership, or a staff function assigned on a part-time basis.

2. A SPECIALIZED GROUP

Such a group is working, preferably full time, at productivity improvement.

3. A MIX OF COMPANY WIDE AND SPECIALIZED GROUP

This can happen for a short period of time only, especially in a large organization, or for a specific project.

Each type of productivity improvement organization requires much thought in order to make it successful, and we shall look next, into some of the factors requiring consideration.

COMPANY WIDE PROGRAM CONSIDERATIONS

1. APPLY EXPERIENCE FROM "NO DIRECT WORK OUTPUT" PROGRAMS

Experience gained from other programs, which are not direct work outputs, can be applied to productivity improvement.

Examples: Safety program, suggestion system, quality of—program.

2. RELIANCE ON COMMITTEES

A company wide program usually relies on committees. It is very difficult to obtain substantial results from a committee, but it can be done.

3. NO POSSIBILITY TO STANDARDIZE PRODUCTIVITY IMPROVEMENT

I have stated before that it is not possible to "standardize" productivity improvement, because it is not possible to standardize management. If it was possible, managers would be replaced by computers.

One well publicized productivity improvement method confirms my "nonstandardization" theory: It is called Quality Circles, and it is, also, one type of committee organization.

Experience indicates that, even in the same corporation, some Quality Circles are effective, while others, set up with the same methods, achieve nothing, and are disbanded.

This means that the success of a program, such as Quality Circles, or Quality of Work Life—in one situation, does not indicate potential success in another situation.

This is true for any improvement method, which works best, and often works only, when designed specifically for the situation.

4. LOSS OF PRODUCTIVE TIME

A substantial loss of productive time can be incurred by employees participating in a committee—or doing related productivity improvement work.

5. WATCH GENERATION OF PAPERWORK

The generation of paperwork must be watched carefully.

Management, or a committee member, may request "another" report, "another plan," without realizing how much work it will require—all outside regular work duties.

Also, excessive time can be spent to insure the accuracy of meeting minutes, and other parliamentary procedures.

6. POSSIBLE "POLITICAL" FUDGING OF RESULTS

Results can be fudged for political reasons, because the same people are formulating productivity improvement, then applying it in their own organizations.

7. PROGRAM ENTHUSIASM MAY FADE WITH TIME

Program enthusiasm and action, may fade with time, since productivity improvement is not the real function of the people doing the work.

8. QUESTIONABLE RESULTS MAY PRECLUDE NEW IMPROVEMENT ACTION

Such a situation may exist for a long time, due to a "we have gone through this before" attitude.

SPECIALIZED GROUP CONSIDERATIONS

1. INTERNAL OR EXTERNAL

The specialized group can be internal or external to the organization.

2. NO LIMITS TO GROUP SIZE

There is no theoretical limit as to size of the group: One person and up.

The group size depends on the magnitude of the project, and the size and means of the organization served.

3. GROUP FULL-TIME FUNCTION?

In the case of an internal group, productivity improvement is not necessarily the full-time group function, or responsibility.

4. OTHER GROUP FUNCTIONS?

Other internal group functions should not impede productivity improvement work. This would happen if management assigns first priority to projects other than productivity improvement. It also happens when there is a conceptual error in the structure, or charter of the specialized group organization.

For example, many Governments include a "Budget and Management" department. Such a department works full time on budget preparation during one part of the year. Then, during the "slack" budget season, Budget and Management is supposed to help, or guide, operating departments in improvement projects.

This is an impossible situation, because during budget preparation, budget and operating departments are in an adversary position, one side pleading for "more," while the other side replies "you can do with less."

Suppose an operating department anticipates a budget cut, which would create an excessive work load. A supervisor may boost, somehow, real resource needs, so that after budget cut—a work load problem is avoided. After budget time, if the Budget and Management department sends an Analyst to the operating department, to work on productivity improvement—how much open cooperation can be expected?

5. SKILLS

The skills required in a specialized productivity improvement group were described previously, in the section on "Productivity improvement work: The worker."

6. ORGANIZATION LOCATION

Finally, like for any internal or external consulting work, it is best for the group to report to the highest possible level of management.

MIXED ORGANIZATION CONSIDERATIONS

If an organization should have productivity improvement activities generated both by a specialized group, and a company wide program, all previous factors should be taken into considerations, with one more, very important:

> For all groups and persons involved: Specific definition of responsibilities, for the formulation and implementation of productivity improvement.

PRODUCTIVITY IMPROVEMENT WORK ORGANIZATION — CONCLUSION

In line with a theme of my productivity improvement lectures, it would be a mistake—to spend excessive time discussing or planning productivity improvement activities.

What is important, is to perform the productivity improvement work—within an organization framework appearing to be best suited for the situation.

As the work proceeds, improvement activities organization, and personnel requirements, will become more and more obvious.

Also, it is important—for upper management, to accept—that it is normal for a productivity improvement function to need improvement too, and that improvement always implies change.

The main aspects of productivity improvement work organization are summarized in the following table.

TABLE XII   PRODUCTIVITY IMPROVEMENT WORK ORGANIZATION

1. COMPANY WIDE PROGRAM

1.1   Similar to "no direct work output programs"
1.2   Relies on committees
1.3   Standardized improvement methods not reliable
1.4   Employees involved lose productive time
1.5   Danger of excessive paperwork
1.6   Possible fudging of improvement results
1.7   Enthusiasm for improvement may fade
1.8   Questionable results may preclude further work

2. SPECIALIZED GROUP

2.1   Can be internal or external
2.2   Group size depends on circumstances
2.3   Productivity full-time group function?
2.4   Other group functions can conflict with productivity improvement work
2.5   Experience (not necessarily with the organization or its type of activity) and CREATIVITY are the main skills required
2.6   Should report to high management level

3. MIXED ORGANIZATION

3.1   Specialized group and other employees work together on improvement program
3.2   Typical "project" or "matrix" organization
3.3   Tasks and individual responsibilities must be well defined

TABLE XII—NOTES

1. Any of the above should be adapted to the improvement situation.

2. Rigid organization concepts are contrary to productivity improvement.

RECURRENT SOURCES OF LOW PRODUCTIVITY

Improper utilization of any resource, or undesirable output, are sources of low productivity.

The same holds true for certain factors, which can be one aspect of a resource, or one aspect of an output.

Practical experience indicates that some of the same sources of low productivity tend to develop, on a recurrent basis, in many types of organization. A review of such "sources" is of value to any person concerned with productivity improvement.

It should be noted that any of the sources of low productivity described next—may, or may not be present in a given organization. Each type of work activity tends to develop its own recurrent low productivity patterns, for which management should be aware, and watchful.

RECURRENT SOURCES OF LOW PRODUCTIVITY

1. PREJUDICE

The first recurrent source of low productivity to keep in mind is "prejudice." It does not mean that it is the most important.

In fact, a generalized classification, and ranking of the many sources of low productivity would make little sense.

Looking at prejudice, in its legal, regulatory , or moral aspects, is not considered, although it may have an effect on productivity, for example by affecting the morale of an organization.

One prejudicial situation I have witnessed time and again, is that of an executive selecting one employee for promotion. If the employee selected is not the one with the best capabilities, the result is a negative effect on the organization's productivity.

Counterproductive prejudice can also be present on a "wholesale" basis, by setting hiring standards eliminating categories of valuable employees.

One study of retiring Chief Executive Officers of medium-sized corporations, showed that they tend to select, for replacement, a person of similar schooling, and similar height as their own.

Personnel height prejudice provides an interesting example, with the assumption that a police officer must be tall—to be effective.

In New York City, the Puerto Rican population had reached one half-million, and the police department still did not have one Puerto Rican national in its ranks.

It took a reduction in personnel height requirements, to have New York City policemen—capable of effectively communicating with the population in Puerto Rican neighborhoods.

RECURRENT SOURCES OF LOW PRODUCTIVITY

2. EQUIPMENT

Henry Ford said:

> "If you need a piece of equipment but don't buy it, you pay for it, even though you don't have it."

This statement is even more valid now than half a century ago, because of the increased importance of "equipment" in most work processes—to the point where certain work processes rely completely on equipment.

Computerized "robots" are a popularized picture of the increased reliance on equipment. However, "automated" production processes (i.e. for metal working) were in use long before the first computer was built—which means that equipment has been a major productivity factor for a long time.

For example, an electronic tube is a high precision assembly of many parts, sealed in a vacuum. The manufacturing of electronic tubes was completely automatic before the word "automation" was coined, and when they were known as "radio" tubes, because commercial television was still a science fiction dream. The most tragic example of the relationship between equipment and productivity—is that of steel companies which failed to modernize their equipment. Foreign companies with modern plants can absorb shipping costs, and still sell at a price lower than what obsolete plants are producing. The argument, or excuse of foreign price support is defeated by modern American steel plants, who can beat any foreign competition.

On the other hand, there is a trend, for American companies who established manufacturing facilities in foreign countries, in order to benefit from lower prevalent wages, to bring back their manufacturing to the United States. The reason is, that improved equipment reduces labor resource requirements, to the point where "labor" is but a small percentage of total production costs.

The increasing importance of equipment confirms why it is obsolete to think in terms of "Labor Productivity," instead of "Organization Productivity."

Also, it indicates why great attention should be given to the EQUIPMENT RESOURCE FACTOR, because of its major, and direct effect on productivity.

RECURRENT SOURCES OF LOW PRODUCTIVITY

3. COMPUTER SYSTEMS

Computers have generated some of the greatest productivity advances, in factories, offices, research, engineering, and many other activities. Yet, it is not unusual to find that a new computer system has reduced productivity.

The reduction in productivity is easily noticed, when the new system requires an increase in personnel, or results in a rate reduction of the organization's work output.

The "new" computer system can be:

    (a) A manual system converted to a computer system, or

    (b) An existing computer system converted to a new computer system.

The productivity problem, with a new computer system, can be of several types:

1. A TRANSITIONAL PRODUCTIVITY PROBLEM

This is a normal occurrence during the installation, and early work period of any new system. However, the reduction in productivity should be anticipated, and provisions made to minimize the effect of the problem, for example with the temporary assignment of additional employees.

2. AN ESTABLISHED PRODUCTIVITY PROBLEM

If, after a reasonable break in, or "debugging" period, the transitional productivity problem does not go away, one must conclude that there is something wrong with the new computer system.

The next course of action should follow principles similar to the solution of any productivity problem: Analysis, identification, solution development and analysis, correction program development and implementation.

In some cases, it may be found that the new system cannot be corrected, or would require excessive resources for correction. At this point, the situation should be analyzed, to decide if scuttling the new system is the most sensible solution.

3. A NEW PRODUCTIVITY PROBLEM

Sometimes, a new computer system creates productivity problems which did not exist before. For example, new "interface" problems, whereby an organization "other" than the organization where the new system was installed—has to do more work because of the new system.

Again, an improvement program should be developed to solve this new productivity problem.

SYSTEM PRODUCTIVITY PROBLEM PREVENTION

The best answer to the new computer system problem is, of course, to prevent it. This should be done during the analysis and planning stages of the new system.

First, and to repeat earlier statements, the "computer system" must be looked at as one element of a broader "system" including all the organizations or activities affected by the computer system. In a broader sense, the computer system is but one "specific system" of the "Comprehensive Management System," including procedures, policy, and organization. I have solved productivity problems appearing to be "computer problems" while the real problem had nothing to do with the computer system. Also, computer system problems which could not be corrected until one element of the broader system was changed, such as a procedure.

Productivity considerations should be a required "task" during the analysis and planning process of any new system. In other words, the following question should be answered:

"How will the new system affect current productivity in our organization, and in interfacing organizations?"

The answer to that question should be carefully evaluated, because a new system may require productivity losses in some areas, in order to benefit from an overall productivity gain.

A new computer system not allowing an overall gain in organization productivity, is a waste of the wonderful possibilities offered by computers. And of course, a waste of capital resources.

RECURRENT SOURCES OF LOW
PRODUCTIVITY

4. PERSONNEL TURNOVER

In any organization, unnecessary costs are a negative productivity factor, and such is the case for personnel turnover.

The direct costs of personnel turnover are easy to measure: Recruiting, hiring, training, learning period, and related personnel activity costs.

While the indirect costs of personnel turnover are difficult to evaluate, they do represent a significant negative productivity factor, by the effect on organization morale, on relations with other internal and external organizations, by the reduction in "experience capital" accumulated in the organization.

Example. An industrial salesman telling me:

"One problem with the XYZ Company, is that you never know whom you will find behind a desk."

The highest—relative—reduction in productivity,

comes from management personnel turnover. While one new worker is learning, the output quantity and quality of that one position is reduced. But when a new manager is learning, inexperienced executive decisions will affect the output of many workers.

Direct costs of turnover have been estimated many times, and the figures are high. However, a comprehensive study of all consequences of personnel turnover, and their cost, may not have been done yet.

One specific, interesting example, was published in the financial magazine Forbes, in its January 2, 1984 issue. It is a short "Trend" item, appropriately titled "More for less."

"Part-time help has for many years been a way of life in the banking business. At the Provident Bank of Cincinnati, for example, 15% of the tellers were part-timers. But with the advent of automatic teller machines at Provident in 1977 and their phenomenal growth during the past three years, the bank needed more and more part-timers. That was a problem. "A lot of people simply won't work for $4 or $5 an hour," says Provident's director of personnel Stuart Mahlin. Also, he says, many part-timers keep hunting full time jobs, so turnover is very high and so are hiring and training costs. So the Provident made a radical move; it decided to pay part-timers more money for less work. A "Peak Time Pay" teller, for example, gets $8.72 an hour for four hours and three days a week, and $9.39 an hour for three hours three days a week. The result? Provident has cut 90,000 working hours at 30 branches, avoided laying off 40 full-timers, lowered the costs and completely changed its applicant base. "We have more men, and people in their 30s, 40s and 50s instead of 20s," says Mahlin, "and they are from a much different social, economic and educational background." Since "Peak Time" was put into place eight months ago, the bank has no part-time turnover and almost no absenteeism. The program has been so successful, in fact, that about 450 other banks and S & Ls are asking the Provident to set up their own peak time program."

This example indicates increased productivity resulting from a reduction in personnel turnover.

There is another interesting and very important fact in this case: Reduction in turnover, therefore increase in productivity followed an increase in salary. This is contrary to recent management policy trends seeking a reduction in salaries to increase productivity.

It is interesting that companies with high turnover tend to have a low reputation in their industry.

On the other hand, companies with low turnover tend to have a good reputation for the quality of their output, and do attract good employees. Even in good economic times, such companies have a long waiting list of potential employees, while Labor Unions organizing efforts usually meet with little success.

One other aspect of personnel turnover, is to create temporary labor shortages, always a costly, counter-productive situation.

The negative impact of turnover can be found in organizations of any size, from a small company—to the United States army. During a talk given at the Commonwealth Club of California, March 21, 1986, on "Military Incompetence," Dr. Richard Gabriel, Consultant to the House and Senate Armed Forces Committees attributed many of the U.S. officers corps problems, all the way to the Joint Chiefs of Staff, to instability: Officers have to move in and out of positions at fast rate in order to retire with a high rank level. In other words, by the time an officer becomes proficient in a given assignment, an inexperienced replacement takes over. It sounded to me like a straightforward turnover productivity problem.

The difficult solutions to the personnel turnover productivity problem can be found only—in the management resources of the organization:

Management policies, management style, and executive talent.

RECURRENT SOURCES OF LOW PRODUCTIVITY

5. PERSONNEL CONTROLS

In any organization, producing widgets, or a service, personnel control activities are not an "output." Therefore, the direct weight of personnel controls on organization productivity is negative.

In his famous book "Parkinson's Law," Professor Parkinson reports one of his research findings, whereby the critical number for an administrative organization is 2,000 employees. When an organization reaches that size, all employees can be working hard, implementing internal controls and procedures, while the organization, as a whole, produces nothing.

Observing some government organizations, where, for example a payroll is arrived at through an incredible amount of "certified" paperwork, does not suggest that such precise controls—contribute to productivity.

Excessive personnel controls generate useless work, lower employee morale, lower productivity.

The most modern management and organization concepts, such as the Volvo assembly plant experiment, or well designed flextime plans, are characterized by a reduction in personnel controls.

Any productivity conscious organization—should optimize its personnel controls, by using the very minimum controls—really required to insure adequate utilization of its personnel resources, under proper financial management.

PERSONNEL CONTROLS

CONTROLS, MORALE, STRESS EXAMPLE

The new director of a 100-employee finance and accounting organization believes in tight controls. To achieve better resources utilization he establishes a "productivity" system requiring each employee, including all management personnel, to write a daily report describing—on an hourly basis—the work done and its location. The daily reports are then keypunched and become the input to a computer system!

Within a few months the organization morale went down. Employees started to leave or seek transfers. One section manager, thirty years with the organization, is probably its most valuable employee. He started to have health problems, until he decided to set a date for early retirement. His health went back to normal.

This example confirms the potential negative results of productivity measurement described earlier. There are many ways to evaluate work activities without using the "stop watch" approach dear to "efficiency experts" of olden days.

RECURRENT SOURCES OF LOW PRODUCTIVITY

6. ORGANIZATION SIZE AND STRUCTURE

During the years, with regard to the size of an organization, two fallacies have characterized public opinion:

(1) Bigger is better.
(2) Smaller is better, stated as "small is beautiful."

The fact is, there is no direct relationship between organization size and productivity. Here are a few reasons.

1. A big organization has access to more capital than a small one, therefore can invest in relatively more productivity improvement equipment. A 10-employee company could not buy a one million Dollars machine. For a giant corporation, it will be a fraction of the yearly capital improvement budget.

2. A small company can move faster than the corporate giants, therefore be more productive.

When I was Chief Engineer of a small 100-employee electronics components company, our competitors were the likes of General Electric and Westinghouse. When a salesman brought in an order for components with a custom specification, our total work time span, through engineering, production, testing, and shipping, was one month. In the same time span, the big corporation may have moved the paperwork through its sales department, and into the engineering department.

3. Then, there is the "management factor": It can be so good, or so bad, that it will outweigh any organization size considerations.

STRUCTURE BIG OR SMALL?

The answer to the organization size dilemma is found through productivity improvement research and analysis, aimed at optimizing the structure of the organization.

For example, in the 1950's, Sears and Roebuck progressed from the image of sleepy small town merchandising, to a highly competitive national retail force. A major success factor was the re-structuring of such a big organization into four management levels only. Once, I had the opportunity to observe how the Sears organization structure affects labor productivity.

I was waiting, while the top of my old Buick Roadmaster convertible was being replaced, in the parking lot of a Los Angeles Sears automotive shop. The worker was friendly, appeared competent, but ran into difficulties. Around 12:15, I told him that if he has to take his lunch break, I will come back later. He answered that "they" trust him to take his lunch break whenever convenient, and that he wants to finish the job.

Soon afterwards, a well dressed gentleman walked into the parking lot, approached and greeted the worker, asked him how he is doing.

After the worker had explained his difficulties, the gentleman got into the car, and while laying on his back, pulling and tucking on the new canvas, discussed with the worker what should be done. After he left, I asked the worker if this was his boss? With a big smile, he answered "No! He is the manager of all Sears Los Angeles area automotive repair shops."

IMPROVED ORGANIZATION CONCEPTS

Both private business and government have displayed slowness, or inertia, in adapting their organization structure to improved productivity concepts.

The successful Volvo assembly plant experiment, whereby a self-managed group of workers is fully responsible for one automobile subassembly, did not spread to other automobile manufacturers.

Except for the aerospace and defense related industries, most organizations are still structured along functional lines.

Relatively few organizations have taken advantage of the "project management" concept—whereby one employee, based in a functional department, works for another, or several other project departments.

One possible reason for uneasiness towards project organization, has to do with promotions, and salary increase practices. Too often, an employee is promoted on the basis of a good relationship with a manager, rather than for actual job performance.

—Not all my productivity improvement efforts turned into successful case histories.

I remember spending long hours with a young government executive, explaining how the project management and control concepts would benefit his department, and solve specific problems affecting the whole organization.
The reaction was positive. However, our work session concluded with the statement—that such a change should take place—at some future time.

Since then, the same person changed jobs a couple of times, and is now in a very high government management position.

ORGANIZATION STRUCTURE AND RESPONSIBILITIES

One productivity problem, found mostly in large organizations, has to do with the distribution of responsibilities between staff and operating functions.
If "politics" plays a bigger role than logic in the assignment of tasks and responsibilities between staff and operations personnel—problems are bound to arise in the management levels, with resulting negative productivity effects on the whole organization.

The relationship between organization structure and productivity—indicates how important it is to develop the optimum structure for each organization.

While considering organization structure changes, it should be remembered that the implementation of any organization change can create a temporary situation of lower productivity.

LECTURE CONCLUSION

Fortunately, most of my productivity improvement efforts did have a successful conclusion.

It is of interest that, in some of my improvement case histories, no more than an "organization structure" change was required to solve the productivity problem.

Except for my time, the implementation cost was zero.

Therefore, it can be stated—that ORGANIZA-TION is a precious source of "no cost" productivity improvement.

During the next lecture, we shall continue the review of Recurrent Sources of Low Productivity.

Thank you.

LECTURE 7

PRODUCTIVITY: IMPROVEMENT MANAGEMENT PRINCIPLES

SUMMARY:
Description of 20 recurrent sources of low productivity, continued. Major requirements for productivity improvements. Bialek's "productivity laws."

INTRODUCTION

Ladies and Gentlemen:

During the previous lecture, we have reviewed six recurrent sources of low productivity.

We shall now review a few more, starting with OVERTIME.

RECURRENT SOURCES OF LOW PRODUCTIVITY

7. OVERTIME

Occasional overtime is generally a positive productivity factor, especially when employees are motivated to achieve an exceptional output goal.

The productivity problem occurs—in organizations afflicted with "chronic" overtime requirements.

The "superman," or "wonderwoman" myth should be recognized as such. Even professional athletes, world champions, get tired. Employees subjected to permanent, excessive overtime will, eventually, suffer from physical and mental fatigue, resulting in lower productivity.

Sometimes, lower productivity due to excessive overtime can have dangerous consequences, as indicated by studies of certain occupations, such as air traffic controllers.

With management personnel, a drastic drop in productivity is often described as "burn-out." Chronic, excessive overtime is, with little doubt, a contributing burn-out factor.

Of course, premium pay for overtime increases resource costs, thus building into the organization a negative productivity factor.

An organization with rare requirements for overtime reflects good planning, and sound management. Such an organization is avoiding—at least one—source of low productivity problems.

RECURRENT SOURCES OF LOW PRODUCTIVITY

8. PROGRESS REPORTING

If progress reporting is a contractual requirement, it is an output. However, "internal" progress reporting required by the procedures of an organization, is not an output, therefore, the work spent on such activity is a negative productivity factor. The obvious conclusion is that it should be kept to a minimum.

Many managements require "scheduled" progress reporting, which is, in most cases, meaningless. An organizational unit, or an employee, is supposed to perform a certain function. As long as the work is performed, without problem for the organization, there is no point in generating paperwork stating:

"The work we were supposed to do—was done."

In the case of projects and tasks, the "binary output" reporting concept, described in a previous lecture, is the most useful: A task is "fully" completed, or is "not fully" completed. Reporting 50%, or other "%" completion, is useful for planning purpose. However, a possibly harsh, but realistic top management appraisal, is to consider—only—the binary progress reports:

"No completion" and "100% completion."

Excessive emphasis on progress reporting reduces management control, because of a natural tendency to make reports "pleasing" to upper management.

On the contrary, EXCEPTION progress reporting provides effective management control, since it calls attention to a problem, or to unusual good performance.

RECURRENT SOURCES OF LOW
PRODUCTIVITY

9. MANAGEMENT STYLE

The management style topic has been written up in several hundred books and articles. Trying a short summary of its important productivity implications is not possible. Therefore, bringing attention to the relationship between management style and productivity will be done with a few comments only.

One aspect of management style is associated with a dilemma, usually described as the "carrot or stick" principles. The answer to that dilemma has not been settled yet, although the trend seems to lean towards the "carrot."

When an organization, a company, is in trouble, it may be a natural reaction to look for a "tough" new manager, who will straighten out the situation.

Business publications abound with admiring stories of the tough new president or chief executive officer taking charge of a troubled corporation. During the first few weeks, he fires half the executives, and warns the balance that they must improve the performance of their departments by so much per month, or else. One year later, an updated story about the same corporation, usually tells that its troubles got worse, and that the board of directors has invited the new leader to pick up his options, and leave.

Many years of my observations in a wide range of organization types, leaves little doubt that an autocratic or authoritarian style of management is detrimental to productivity. Some of the negative effects I have witnessed are mentioned in the listing of resource factors in Lecture #4: Lower morale, motivation, loyalty, and "secret attitude." Furthermore, subordinates seldom dare criticizing a detrimental management policy or decision.

Autocratic management is counterproductive. Such a fact applies to any management situation, from a small company to a big corporation, and even to the government of a nation. For example, World War II history recorded how many wrong decisions by German leadership could not be challenged, even by generals. We should be grateful for the negative autocratic factor. Otherwise, the flag flying over our government buildings—could be other than the American flag.

RECURRENT SOURCES OF LOW PRODUCTIVITY

10. WORK ENVIRONMENT

Managements underestimating the productivity value of an adequate work environment is a matter of great amazement.

Inadequate facilities, and uncomfortable environment, make the work more difficult, increase fatigue, create employee dissatisfaction, reduce loyalty, and lower productivity.

The first word processing equipments, installed without attention to glare, seating comfort, and noise, created so much resentment amongst feminist organizations, that one hears about it yet.

From multiple work environment mistakes I have witnessed, here are a few examples.

EXAMPLE 1

In Los Angeles, where there is a great need for air conditioning to compensate for the lack of insulation in industrial buildings, management of that company was saving on its utility bills by recycling the same indoor air through a cooling system.

By early afternoon, indoor air pollution was worth than outside during a smog alert. Employees located near a window would open it a little, to let some hot but cleaner air in, while watching out for top management, since opening windows was against the rules.

When the air started to feel really bad, most employees would "make believe" they are working, while sipping soft drinks, and complaining.

On any hot days, for two or three hours in the afternoon, productivity was close to zero.

EXAMPLE 2

One group I was working with was relocated, on a temporary basis, in half a warehouse type building. The other half was used by a wholesale company. The partition between the two warehouse tenants was a plain plywood wall.

On certain days, a strange thing was happening to our group: We felt drowsy. After lunch, some employees were falling asleep. The bottom line was, that on such days, very little work got done.

Because, on such days, a faint smell was in the air, our corporate plant management went to investigate what was going on in the other side of the building. It turned out to be a wholesale pharmaceutical company, storing basic ingredients in barrels, and other huge containers.

The employees were taking the ingredients from a big container to fill small containers, sold to pharmacies. One or two days a week, they were handling a powder stored in barrels. That powder was a basic ingredient for calming and relaxing medications. It must have been effective, because just smelling it was putting us to sleep.

Sealing the cracks in the plywood partition improved the work environment—and our performance. Further improvement resulted from moving to a better building.

EXAMPLE 3

In June 1983, I witnessed an unbelievable work environment blunder.

The big chain supermarket where we did most of our shopping at that time, had installed new check-out stands, with laser scanning equipment. I was curious to see how much faster the checker is working, and observed the action while waiting in a check-out line.

First, the checker had to move a package several times over the scanning device to obtain a reading, and she had to give up for about one out of two times. Well, this was a bug in the system, which could probably be fixed.

Then, I noticed that to punch an amount on the register, the checker had to reach over the shopping cart being checked out, and that the keys were at her head level, which means that her arm was extended all the way, perpendicular to her body.

When our turn came, and because she was one of our usual checkers, I asked her what she thought of the register keyboard location. "Terrible" was her answer, "but look at the scale." I could not have seen the scale platform while I was in line, because it was located flush against the wall of the counter, where the customer is standing during check-out.

The checker showed me that by bending over, with her arm extended all the way, she could touch the scale platform. I told her that by handling weights in that position, she could hurt her back. She answered that she did already. Then she added: "When I have to weigh a watermelon, it is impossible, I have to walk around."

One point to consider in such a situation, in addition to the direct, obvious impairment of productivity, is how employees feel about management, and what it does to labor relations. Consulting with a few employees—who may have never heard about industrial engineering— would have avoided such mistakes.

Second point, this took place in a major corporation. Does it tell something about potential productivity problems in corporate managements?

Third point, when employees are given the wrong work environment, who is responsible for lower productivity: Labor, or management?

Fourth point, it is well over half a century, since Frank Gilbreth, and other pioneers of scientific management, demonstrated how a work station designed for ease and comfort increases productivity.

While a new discipline, "ergonomics," also called "human factors engineering," made into a science the adaptation of environment to human work needs, common sense, and utilization of workers' experience, can do a lot—to design work environments conducive to productivity improvement.

Fifth point, the nagging question is: "Why does not management use existing, proven knowledge related to work environment?"

This question leads us into the next recurrent source of low productivity, "re-inventing the wheel."

RECURRENT SOURCES OF LOW PRODUCTIVITY

11. RE-INVENTING THE WHEEL

Useless waste of resources, and counterproductive actions, are, besides other reasons, the result of people re-inventing the wheel. While this is done in many activities, we are concerned with productivity improvement management.

Re-inventing the wheel is a waste, because if something has been worked out before, there is no point in going through the development process again. Then, if mistakes have been made in the past, there is no point in repeat performances.

A good, or bad productivity management action, may not have the same effects in a different setting, or situation.

For example, a new executive may order actions which seem proper, because the same actions, taken in the previous job, worked wonders—for the previous organization, under different conditions. The results of such actions can be different in the new organization.

Instead of imposing principles carried over from the previous organization—analysis, interviews with old-time employees, may reveal that similar actions taken in the past had adverse consequences. Such knowledge will help reshape a new course of action, and make it successful.

Ignoring the general "state-of-the-art," or more directly, what was done before, and worked, or did not work, will result not only in wasted efforts, but in costly blunders.

In the previous section on work environment, the poorly designed supermarket check-out station was a good example of wheel re-inventing.

A huge body of industrial engineering literature is available in many libraries. The knowledge is available. Why not use it?

This reminds me of a great French playwright, actor, director, and wit, named Sacha Guitry, who said:

"Why go to school, when all human knowledge can be found in books?"

Research, oriented towards what was written and done before, towards an evaluation of current state-of-the art, should not be limited to scientific work.

In an organization concerned with the management of productivity, properly conducted research is, a highly productive activity. It will avoid waste, and other negative productivity factors.

Avoidance of re-inventing the wheel should not be confused with the avoidance of trying something new. As stated in a previous lecture, the concepts of "conservatism" and "productivity improvement" are not compatible.

RECURRENT SOURCES OF LOW PRODUCTIVITY

12. RELIANCE ON WRITTEN PROCEDURES

Suppose an executive states: "Our problem is that we do not have enough procedures." In such a situation, there is a high probability that the organization has one, or many productivity problems—which are not the lack of written procedures.

On the other hand, if an excessive usage of procedures is required to perform a given function—this too indicates a productivity problem, such as, a system which could use some simplification.

Written procedures are necessary to develop and install a new system. Then, the "ideal" system should be so simple and easy to use—that there is no need for the written procedures.

NOTE

Procedures should still be maintained and updated for systems documentation.

RECURRENT SOURCES OF LOW PRODUCTIVITY

13. CUMBERSOME PROCEDURES

The words PROCEDURES, METHODS, PROCESS, are used in different organizational settings. For the productivity improvement management outlook, we can assume the same meaning: "How" the work, a given task, is accomplished. However, "cumbersome" procedures have the greatest tendency to develop in administrative settings, rather than in a manufacturing setting were wasteful actions are more obvious.

The worse set of administrative procedures I have ever seen, was in a series of company manuals filling several standard bookcase shelves. Some of the procedures went on for 70 pages. (See note below).

The worst individual procedure I have ever seen was a procedure listing the verbs to be used in writing procedures.

Good written procedures are short, easy to understand by a new employee, easy to remember, and have been recently updated—let us say no more than one year ago.

The best procedures I have seen, were hidden somewhere on the desk of an old-time employee. Usually, one or two sheets, covered with notes, telling all there is to know about the functions assigned to that position. The same employee may display the company manual in its fancy binder, but will almost never use it. The good systems and procedures professional will establish a trustful relationship with such employees. This will benefit the productivity of the systems and procedures function, and will make its output a more productive resource for the organization.

Also, the good systems and procedures professional should refrain his or her pride of authorship for the written word—in favor of pride of authorship for a really good system.

HOW GOOD PROCEDURES BECOME CUMBERSOME

A new procedure is developed, installed, "debugged," and works well. Then, a new requirement comes up, and the procedure is changed. Then, a new executive comes in, and imposes a principle which worked wonders in his or her previous job: The procedure is changed. After a few years of piecemeal changes, the procedure is cumbersome.

Furthermore, requirements external to the organization where the work process takes place, may not have been incorporated in the procedure, because it could be too difficult.

The description above is a typical productivity problem situation. The solution is to develop and install a new procedure.

It should be remembered that even with employees involvement, a must, and unanimous agreement that the new procedure is good—some errors will be made. Blaming one person or another would be a bigger mistake. Fine tuning the new procedure is part of the implementation process.

During a productivity survey, it is worth-while looking at the latest publication date of a written procedure. While this is not a sure proof test, if the latest date is over one year old, there is a good probability that the procedure is in need of improvement.

> "Streamlining procedures" is an effective and usually "no cost" productivity improvement method. I have used it successfully many times.

NOTE

It would be presumptuous to state that there is a direct relationship between lengthy, cumbersome procedures, and the demise of a business. Many factors lead to that. However . . .

After I had reviewed the written procedures of that company, employing several thousand employees, the executive in charge did not disagree with my opinion. But he did not retain my services to improve the procedures either.

Shortly thereafter, the company started to loose money at an increasing rate, and was eventually absorbed by a conglomerate.

RECURRENT SOURCES OF LOW PRODUCTIVITY

14. MEETINGS

The relationship between meetings and organization productivity is a good example of the "reasonable" concept, which does not lend itself to rigorous definitions, but is, nevertheless, associated with important productivity factors.

What is a reasonable meeting frequency? It must be determined through experience.

Too many meetings is a negative productivity factor, because it takes too much time away from regular work functions.

Not enough meetings is also a negative productivity factor, because meetings are a good way to maintain communications between employees who do not have constant work contacts, and also a quick way to discuss and solve current work problems.

How much preparation?

Not enough meeting preparation is a negative productivity factor, since participants did not have a chance to think about the topics to be discussed, to do the necessary research work.

General Joffre was commander in chief of the French army during World War I, from 1914 to 1916. He applied timeless management principles, always starting a meeting with the sentence: "De quoi s'agit-il?" which translates: "What is it all about?" This was a reminder to his staff that the agenda and objectives of a meeting must be clear and well defined.

Excessive meeting preparation, such as advance mailing of all the material to be presented, is a loss of time, and can create the great speaker ego-chattering experience: Watching an audience falling asleep.

The style of meeting leadership and control is an important factor, treated in books on communications.

The work environment factor is as important for meetings, as for any work situation. This too has been extensively studied and written up. For example, the effect of seating arrangement on the meeting participants is a fascinating subject.

The most interesting example I know, regarding the relationship between work environment, and the outcome of a meeting, took place in New York, under the administration of Mayor La Guardia.

One municipal labor union was on strike. Mayor La Guardia called the labor and management leaders to a meeting, at a strange address. As the meeting participants arrived, they found that this was an old abandoned government building. This was winter time, in New York, and the building had no heat, no furniture. When all invited were in, Mayor La Guardia locked the door, put the key in his pocket, and announced that they will be standing in the cold room—until the strike is settled. The strike was settled.

Some of the negative meeting productivity factors I
have witnessed the most often, are:

Disturbing noises, interruptions, and no advance
knowledge of the agenda. Of course, there are more.

Improving the productivity of meetings is not
difficult: A little planning, a checklist (who is
bringing the slides?), and a minimum of leadership ability—will do it.

RECURRENT SOURCES OF LOW PRODUCTIVITY

15. TELEPHONE AND WRITTEN COMMUNICATIONS

American Telephone and Telegraph does a great job, advertising how executives can improve their productivity with increased use of the telephone. Well, incalculable losses of productivity are caused—by excessive use of the telephone.

Some executives, and employees, are "always" on the telephone, while people are waiting for them, in and out of their offices.

The way to analyze such a productivity problem is through work sampling. Sometimes, the problem is so overwhelming, that informal observations are sufficient to provide clear problem identification. Otherwise, the formal and well established work sampling techniques (available in the literature) will define the level of the problem.

The work sampling results can be computed into two ratios:

RATIO 1 = TELEPHONE TIME / OTHER TASKS TIME

RATIO 2 = PRODUCTIVE TELEPHONE TIME /
TOTAL TELEPHONE TIME

Unless the organization is a telephone sales group, in general, the problem is with the second ratio.

Productivity increases when employees learn how to increase the ratio of productive telephone time over total telephone time.

The secret, to understand counterproductive telephone and communications practices, can be found in the theoretical scientific research work done, by coincidence, at the Bell Laboratories, by Claude E. Shannon.

In July 1948, Shannon published in the Bell System Technical Journal, a paper titled "A Mathematical Theory of Communication," which became the basic reference of modern communication and information theory.

Before going into the mathematical derivations, which can be followed only by people who studied for an advanced science degree, Shannon shows the basic principle of communication, in the form of a block-diagram.

Slightly simplified, the following block-diagram indicates how the signal of a "transmitted message" is mixed with "noise" to result in a "received message" signal.

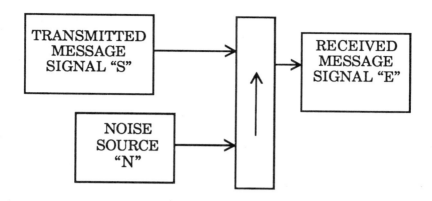

Fig. 6 Basic communication process

Shannon's basic equation of the communication process is:

$$E = f(S, N)$$

The received signal "E", is a function of the transmitted signal "S", and noise "N".

Since we are not worried about obtaining a good grade in mathematics, but are trying to derive the practical implications of this very important theory—for productivity management purpose—we shall be satisfied with the following communication theory equation:

**TRANSMITTED MESSAGE + NOISE =
RECEIVED MESSAGE**

One more point of theory. "NOISE" in our communication equation has two meanings:

1. Real noise, such as a jack-hammer going nearby.

2. Words, sentences, or other communication items, having nothing to do with the "TRANSMITTED MESSAGE."

   For example, a person calls to set up a business meeting, then proceeds to tell, in great detail, what happened during last week-end's fishing trip.

   Words and sentences pertaining to the business meeting are the TRANSMITTED MESSAGE.

   The week-end story is NOISE. Static in the telephone line, people speaking loudly nearby are NOISE.

   Any type of NOISE reduces the reliability, the quality of the RECEIVED MESSAGE.

In written communications, an illustration of our communication theory equation is to use several pages—to state what should be written in a few lines.

Noise, in any type of communications, can be looked at as waste. Therefore, it is a negative productivity factor—to be carefully avoided.

RECURRENT SOURCES OF LOW PRODUCTIVITY

16. WORK ASSIGNMENTS

In general, low productivity associated with work assignments results from a task, or function, assigned to the wrong person.

The task may not be assigned to the most qualified employee in the organization. Or it may be assigned to a highly competent employee who lacks some specific qualifications required for that task.

Out of my experience, witnessing poor productivity resulting from wrong employee work assignment—one case stands out:

The best and most productive computer programmer I have known. For example, in a meeting including several other senior programmers and analysts, called for the purpose of solving 10 computer system problems, while she was working out problem No. 6, the other programmers were still trying to reach a comfortable understanding of her solution to problem No. 3.

Well, upper management decided that she should engage in management analysis work, with the idea of finding computer solutions—after identifying the management problems.

It was a pathetic, sad performance, because of a total lack of experience, and lack of interest in management work. Not only was the productivity value of that assignment zero, the company had registered a loss of valuable professional time.

This was one example, of extremely low productivity resulting from the wrong work assignment.

On the positive side of my observations—I have solved productivity problems—simply by convincing management to change the structure of organizational responsibilities. This is standard "no cost" improvement.

For remedial action, it is important to consider why such productivity problems occur. Some of the reasons are as follows:

(1) **Making the wrong assumptions.** A person proven outstanding at several types of work assignments may not necessarily succeed with a new one.

(2) **Politics.** This is one of the most frequent causes of the productivity problem. A person is selected for a new work assignment—on the basis of on-the-job friendship, or of having something in common with a manager, such as a previous place of employment, a club, a college, a birthplace, etc.

(3) **Management style.** Close to "politics." In a dictatorship, industrial and other institutions controlled by the government are led by managers selected within the premise of political conformity. Comparing the economic development of such countries against the free world provides obvious answers.

Back to my own practical experience, I have witnessed one further counterproductive result of wrong work assignments: The organization may loose a valuable employee.

Like for so many other management actions, before making a work assignment decision, the vital question should be asked:

"What will be the effect on organization productivity?"

RECURRENT SOURCES OF LOW PRODUCTIVITY

17. PLANNING

Like for so many other organization productivity resource factors, planning requires optimization. "Adequate" planning is a positive productivity factor. However, planning becomes a negative factor, when it is insufficient, or excessive.

In most cases, the productivity problem is with insufficient planning. It can be found in all types and sizes of organizations.

One interesting example can be found in the book titled "On a Clear Day You Can See General Motors," when John de Lorean describes the effect of lack of top management planning at General Motors, during the '70s. For example, one study indicated that getting tooling programs into shops—on time, would add $550 million to General Motor's yearly profit.

On the other hand, too much planning is a productivity loss, because planning is not an organization output. In extreme cases, it can interfere with real work, to the point where little or no work gets done.

In one extreme case I have witnessed, the head of a newly formed analysis group would not let his personnel start work on any of several proposed projects, until upper management approved a total, comprehensive plan. For one reason or another, management did not get around to approving the long range plan. Eventually, the group was disbanded, having accomplished nothing, except planning.

One historical example of excessive planning preventing productive action, could be challenged, on the basis that failure was caused by intentional political motives. Nevertheless, it did happen, and did have adverse consequences still affecting the world today.

One or two years after the end of World War II, a 3-day, 4-Power conference took place in Paris. The conference was at the Head of Department of State level, with delegations from the United States, Russia, England, and France.

The conference had been called to smooth out mounting East-West frictions, and problems.

Once, I found myself in a street used by the delegations on their way to the conference. The organizers, no doubt diplomats, had made sure to have each delegation riding in exactly the same type and number of cars, with the same formation of police cars and motorcycles. The only difference from one motorcade to another, was the two small national flags flying on the front fenders of the lead limousines.

Well, the first day of the conference was devoted to planning the agenda. This was the gist of the official communiqué.

The second day communiqué stated that no agreement had been reached on setting the agenda. The third and last day conference communiqué announced that no agreement could be reached on an agenda, and the meeting was adjourned.

This 4-Power conference, where all the work done was planning only, was a complete failure.

Regardless of political motives, if the participants would have started negotiating, instead of planning, the outcome might have been different.

The reaction of the people of Paris, starved for peace, was sad. However, we did know that this conference failure was leading into the "cold war," which started soon afterwards.

How much planning is right?

We could imagine a concept, whereby in a given organization, there is an optimum ratio, between planning work, and productive work.

Spending time to develop an exact figure, an exact ratio—would not be necessarily productive.

However, productivity management does require attention to "adequate" planning.

RECURRENT SOURCES OF LOW PRODUCTIVITY

18. WASTE

Waste—of resources—does exist in every organization. Eliminating waste reduces the cost of resources used to run the organization, therefore increases prodductivity.

Many times, a probably apocryphal story has been told, how a business tycoon had his first break, when he was an office boy: The big boss noticed him picking up a paper clip from the floor, and promoted him to be his staff assistant.

During the ages, dreamers and crooks have attempted to build a perpetual motion machine. It is impossible, because in any machine, there is a loss of energy—waste. Reducing waste increases the efficiency of the machine. This was done for the design of American automobiles, when gasoline mileage became an important marketing factor.

Waste is an integral part of any work process. Some waste is obvious, for example the metal or other material left over after machining operations. Some waste is less obvious, for example a procedure calling for 8 document copies to be made, when 5 only are really needed.

The waste of time resources is obvious when workers

are idle. It is less obvious when workers are very busy, engaging in activities contributing little, or nothing, to the output of the organization.

Too often, the elimination of waste is done on an emergency basis, for example during a budget crisis. Such productivity improvement activities are also a waste, because they are usually done without sufficient analysis. If an organization is faced with a shortage of cash, there may be no other choice, but hurried cost cutting. Otherwise, the long range, overall effect of what is suspected, or designated as "waste" must be carefully studied.

The recapture, or recycling of waste can be a valuable method to increase productivity—if the cost and consequences of such recycling are beneficial.

In previous lectures, I mentioned how recycling heat can increase the productivity of an industrial process. I have read about one paint manufacturing company cutting costs by 2%, by washing down plant floors to recapture spilled pigments.

On the other hand, I have seen several cases of improper recycling of conditioned air, reducing employee work performance.

> One waste reduction "trap" is to confuse savings resulting from a change in policy with savings resulting from a change in procedure. This can happen for most productivity improvement proposals.

An example of procedure is: "Should a lower priced material be used for a work process?"

One example of policy is: "Should the company pay the travel costs of an employee attending a professional society convention?"

Adding "policy" items to a productivity improvement proposal improves the bottom line. However, the long range implication of policy change proposals must be carefully analyzed, and clearly stated.

Productivity minded management should be tolerant of some waste, since it is impossible to run an organization without it. However, constant management attention should be given to waste increase, and to methods of turning waste into a useful resource.

RECURRENT SOURCES OF LOW PRODUCTIVITY

19. EMPLOYEE THEFT

Financial losses reduce the over-all productivity of an enterprise. Employee theft can be a significant negative factor, "comprehensive" because it results from several resource factors reviewed, such as motivation, morale, loyalty, alienation, and corruption.

The current theft losses estimate for the U.S. retail business is $12 billion per year. This does not include theft from other sources, such as shoplifting, and the cost of security.

Sociologists attribute a large extent of the problem to the poor treatment given part-time employees: Low wages, no benefits, and no job security. On the other hand, I have indicated how good treatment of part-time employees can increase productivity. See Recurrent Source of Low Productivity #4, Personnel Turnover.

The employee theft problem is not limited to the retail business. It affects government, and many sectors of industry. One form of the problem is the theft of trade secrets. One typical example I knew, was the chief engineer of a leading electronic company leaving to take a job with the main competitor, and taking with him a suitcase full of blueprints. The actual value of such a theft can be debated, it is an intangible figure. But the cost of lawsuits, countersuits and appeals going on for years is tangible, real.

In manufacturing companies, some employees may steal parts and materials small enough to be hidden in clothing, or find a way to get through a security gate. Besides attention to the resource factors mentioned earlier, one way to reduce such theft is a management policy allowing employees to purchase—at low cost, the parts and materials handled in their work. I have seen such a policy working out well in a large consumer electronics manufacturing company. This was at a time when the repair of a radio or television set involved mostly the replacement of one component. All company technicians did some repair work on the side. They could purchase components from the company, at cost! Because of the volume purchased, the company cost was only a fraction of the price to be paid in a parts store. It was not worth taking a chance to steal when such a bargain was available, and employees felt good towards the company for having such a policy. I would not say that absolutely no theft was going on, but for sure much less than without such a realistic management policy.

After bargain price sale, the next step to prevent employee theft, and associated security costs, is—giving. The by-product of such a policy is to create a good "intangible" work environment, so important for productivity.

One industrialist told me about his young lean days, when he was a waiter in a restaurant. Employee relations were bad. Personnel had to pay for the food eaten. The kitchen was in a basement, a long distance from the dining room. Between kitchen and dining room he would eat a serving of caviar, then go back to argue that his order was not filled. On the other hand, I have known workers allowed to take home for their family food they were handling or producing. The attitude of such workers towards their employers indicate that the "giving policy" is a small price to pay to secure one positive productivity factor.

RECURRENT SOURCES OF LOW PRODUCTIVITY

20. "MEMORANDUMITIS"

"Memorandumitis" is a syndrome, characterized by the compulsion to write and send memos. It can be observed in all types of organizations, from very large to small, in private business and in government.

Why are memoranda counterproductive?

1. They are not an organization work output.
2. They consume productive time.
3. They lengthen the time and structure of communications.
4. They delay operational problems solving.
5. They increase the risk of inter-organizational conflicts.

Lawrence A. Appley was, for many years, President of the American Management Association, and a great teacher of practical management. In his book "The Management Evolution," he wrote:

"The office memorandum is the most costly

management tool for the little it accomplishes and the trouble it creates. An identification of it as "Management Enemy Number One" should be posted on every bulletin board of every business office and plant." (1)

One of so many counterproductive examples I have witnessed, and certainly not the worse, is that of a mature employee, much liked by his fellow employees, whose work was very valuable to the organization. An upper level manager sent him a memo, notifying a change of assignment. This was the first time the employee had heard about the management decision. He did not care for the newly assigned environment, and retired.

The loss to the organization could have been avoided by a meeting, a talk between the manager and the employee, by not using the memo as a means of communication.

If a memo must be written, one should remember the basic theory of communication mentioned in "Source of Low Productivity No. 15, Telephone and Written Communications."

One should make special efforts to avoid "noise," in this case excessive wording.

How many times did I see the recipient of a 3-page memo "suffering"—to come to the end of it. In general, a very few lines could have given the "message." The rest of the 3 pages was "noise."

(1) Lawrence A. Appley, THE MANAGEMENT EVOLUTION, (New York: American Management Association, 1963) p. 191.

One person I worked with had a very wealthy relative. His business was to buy up sections of forest, tree groves, and sell the trees to lumber dealers. He attributed his business success to one management policy:

"Never write a letter, never make a phone call."

Whenever he learned about a potential business deal, buying or selling, and without having the slightest idea how good a prospect it was, he took off, to find out in person.

Of course, there probably were other factors for this businessman's success. But there is no reason to disbelieve that his systematic policy of direct communications was a major factor.

The productivity value of direct communications should be remembered, every time one sits down to write a memo.

RECURRENT SOURCES OF LOW
PRODUCTIVITY

SUMMARY

Well, we have reviewed 20 recurrent sources of low productivity, summarized in the following table. No doubt, more sources of low productivity deserve the same definition.

TABLE XIII   RECURRENT SOURCES OF LOW PRODUCTIVITY

1. Prejudice
2. Equipment
3. Computer systems
4. Personnel turnover
5. Personnel controls
6. Organization size and structure
7. Overtime
8. Progress reporting
9. Management style
10. Work environment
11. Re-inventing the wheel
12. Reliance on written procedures
13. Cumbersome procedures
14. Meetings
15. Telephone and written communications
16. Work assignments
17. Planning
18. Waste
19. Employee theft
20. "Memorandumitis"

NOTES

1. Any type of the sources of low productivity listed may, or may not be present in a given organization.

2. Each type of organization, of work activity, will have its own specific—recurrent—productivity problems.

3. An organization manager—concerned with productivity management—will maintain a list of such recurrent problems, and will, whenever necessary, take preventive action.

PRODUCTIVITY IMPROVEMENT MAJOR REQUIREMENTS

After studying so many aspects of productivity improvement management, it may be useful to review, once more, the major requirements for productivity improvement, as stated in my lecture titled "PRODUCTIVITY: THE ELUSIVE GOLD MINE."

The ten items listed in the following table are based on my own experience, and could not cover all improvement situations.

NOTE

Each organization or activity may have its own specialized requirements.

TABLE XIV   MAJOR REQUIREMENTS FOR PRODUCTIVITY IMPROVEMENT

1. It is necessary to remember that productivity depends on all levels, all aspects of an organization: The assembly line as well as the executive offices, the tangible, such as—a machine, as well as the intangible, such as—a management system—a policy.

2. It is necessary to avoid making assumptions about productivity.

3. It is necessary to avoid the confusion—between appearance of effective work, and real work results.

4. It is necessary to make and sustain a commitment to productivity improvement.

5. It is necessary to thoroughly analyze productivity problems, and productivity improvement opportunities.

6. It is necessary to develop the methods, means, and plans—to achieve productivity improvement, then—to carry out the implementation.

7. It is necessary to accept progress—to seek and make progress.

8. It is necessary to be receptive to new ideas, coming from any source, and applied to any aspect of the organization.

9. It is necessary to accept change. However, any proposed, or planned, or forced change must be analyzed for its effect on productivity.

10. It is necessary to make productivity improvement an integral part of the functions of an organization.

PRODUCTIVITY IMPROVEMENT MANAGEMENT

CONCLUSION

The purpose of these sessions was to communicate, I hope, the essence of my findings, resulting from several years of research on productivity.

That research was based, partly on the literature, and mostly on many—many years of practical observations and experience.

Somehow, that work let me to formulate a few "productivity laws." So far, thirteen.

The statement of my "productivity laws" will be used as conclusion to this lecture series.

BIALEK'S PRODUCTIVITY LAWS

The first "law" was stated in my lecture titled "PRODUCTIVITY: THE ELUSIVE GOLD MINE." It is important enough to mention again, and refers to the subtitle of this book.

FIRST PRODUCTIVITY LAW

(1) Low productivity is—usually—associated with hard work.

To amplify:

(2) Hard work—required—to achieve reasonable output goals—indicates low productivity.

(3) Hard work—not sufficient—to achieve reasonable output goals—indicates a productivity problem.

SECOND PRODUCTIVITY LAW

The well managed organization responds to change through productivity improvement.

THIRD PRODUCTIVITY LAW

Productivity problems go unsolved, due to failure of:

(1) Identifying and defining the problem.

(2) Addressing the real cause of the problem.

FOURTH PRODUCTIVITY LAW

Management productivity—is the main determinant of an organization's productivity.

FIFTH PRODUCTIVITY LAW

On management productivity:

Management, at its best, is a creative process.

SIXTH PRODUCTIVITY LAW

On waste:

Producing or doing anything—cannot be done— without waste.

After reducing waste to a minimum . . .

(1) Wasted material or energy should be recycled.

(2) Wasted work time should be used for productivity improvement.

SEVENTH PRODUCTIVITY LAW

Improvement—is the only useful productivity work activity.

EIGHTH PRODUCTIVITY LAW

A good work procedure is so simple to follow and easy to learn, that there is no need for a written procedure.

> Note: This does not eliminate the need for written procedures documentation.

NINTH PRODUCTIVITY LAW

Re-inventing the wheel—is a counterproductive
work activity.

TENTH PRODUCTIVITY LAW

Next to management, innovation—is the most important factor for productivity improvement.

ELEVENTH PRODUCTIVITY LAW

Any plan, any work, must include a mix of dream
and realism.

Dream only is a cop-out.

Realism only, or practicality only, affords little
chance for major achievement.

TWELFTH PRODUCTIVITY LAW

Organization structures—excessively loose or rigid,
impede productivity improvement.

THIRTEENTH PRODUCTIVITY LAW

Managing change—is an increasingly important part of the management function.

It is, also, another way to describe the management of productivity improvement.

HOW I SOLVED A VARIETY OF PRODUCTIVITY PROBLEMS

Productivity improvement can be achieved in many situations and activities. I have obtained profitable results in a variety of organizational settings, from small company to large corporation, in the private sector and in government. This is illustrated in the following case histories.

NOTE: While the analysis and other phases of a productivity improvement project have been treated at length in the preceding lectures, I have resisted the temptation to classify or list methodology. The text explains it. As stated many times, the number of factors creating a productivity problem situation is great, and the similarity of two problems can be misleading. **The methodology of an effective improvement project must be specific to the situation.**

PRODUCTIVITY IMPROVEMENT CASE HISTORIES

CONTENTS

PRODUCTIVITY IMPROVEMENT CASE HISTORY

TECHNICAL RESEARCH

SUMMARY:
A research project stalled for one year. By cutting across organization lines to tap underutilized talent, the productivity problem was solved in one week.

SETTING: Medium size company, leader in its field.

NOTE: I found no difference between productivity problems occurring in France or in the United States. Similar circumstances and situations result in similar problems.

During the final phases of World War II, the Allied armies moving into Germany captured many top scientists. France landed its prize, a scientist working on microwave technology, a field which started during that period, and was the basis for the development of radar. The scientist's work was so important to the Germans, that his laboratory was located in an isolated estate surrounded by a small army. The French government assigned him to work for that company, at the time the largest manufacturer of electronic test equipment outside the United States. The French Navy needed microwave test equipment for its radar armament program. A "state of the art" Research and Development contract was awarded to the company, with the understanding that a production contract would follow the prototype acceptance tests.

When the company president asked me to look into the problem, I was told that the German scientist had designed a remarkable piece of test equipment, except that it did not pass the Navy acceptance tests, because it did not meet the negotiated specifications. During the following few months, the scientist designed a number of engineering modifications. None worked, and he quit.

I came on the scene one year after the first Navy acceptance test. The project was managed by an electronic staff engineer who did not seem to fit anywhere on the organization chart, except that he was an old and trusted friend of the company president.

While not a novice at engineering, I knew absolutely nothing about microwave technology. However, in talking to the staff engineer about the methods he had been using to tackle the problem, it became apparent to me that his efforts were closer to mechanical rather than electronic engineering.

Now, while making a survey of all professional company personnel, I was especially interested by the case of a young, bright and outspoken mechanical engineer. He was in charge of all draftsmen, and of the toolmakers. He was the real chief mechanical engineer, a title assumed by the manufacturing manager. The mechanical engineer was unhappy with his functional position in the company, and by the lack of attention given to his professional suggestions. All his previous experience had been in the watch industry, and even the precision meters manufactured by the company were "sloppy" engineering for him. He was unhappy. He was considering a change.

While reviewing the project with the electronic staff engineer, I had little doubt that the problem would be an adequate challenge for the mechanical engineer. Furthermore, the staff engineer appeared ready to accept help.

The company president gave me the green light. I talked to the mechanical engineer. As I was leaving his office, he was one happy engineer rolling out clean tracing paper on his huge drafting table.

CONCLUSION

One week later, all the design and engineering modification work was done. The company president was satisfied, and confident enough to call the Navy and request a new acceptance test. One month later, he received his production contract.

No cost was required to implement the productivity problem solution: A change in the project organization. One by-product was to boost the morale of a valuable employee, perhaps prevent his leaving the company.

NOTE ON PRODUCTIVITY IN RESEARCH

PROFESSIONAL EMPLOYEES UTILIZATION

The problem of using professional personnel adequately is a common one. It has nothing to do with time and location. The progressive increase in the number of specialized professional fields may even make it worse.

For example, I have seen many outstanding computer programmers performing badly at systems analysis, and failing completely when assigned tasks closer to the definition of management analysis. On the other hand, in a famous U.S. university research center, scientists of international reputation in many fields, such as chemistry, biology, need computers to analyze experimental laboratory test data. The scientists labor at writing their own computer programs—then have to enlist the services of a programmer I know, to get the programs to work.

I could not quote my friend's comments as to how the

scientists' programs are designed and written, and on the waste of hard to get research funds, when the scientists select computer equipment.

In research, like in any other activity, management attention should be given to assigning a given task to the person most qualified to perform it. This will free research investigators to spend their time on their specialty, therefore increase the probability of higher organization productivity.

PRODUCTIVITY IMPROVEMENT CASE HISTORY

RESEARCH AND DEVELOPMENT

SUMMARY:
A simple method for interpretation of large company policies and procedures—helped engineers and scientists expedite their paperwork, and devote more time to their productive activities.

SETTING: Large aerospace corporation, at the time, recognized U.S. leader in electronics.

One common characteristic of large organizations is a great number of administrative controls, enforced by means of approval or authorization by various management levels.

At the Research and Development laboratories of that corporation, the situation was complicated by the fact that most engineering and scientific activities were organized in a "grid" pattern of functional and project managements.

While experienced secretaries could handle the preparation of routine administrative matters, technical paperwork took up too much engineering time. Then, administrative or technical paperwork had to be approved.

Secretaries, administrators, engineers, supervisors, were too often faced with the question: "Who is supposed to approve a given administrative action?" The answer could be found in several sets of policy and procedures manuals. However, searching for comprehensive answers was time consuming.

Engineers and scientists do not generally like administrative rules. For that reason, figuring out what was really meant by a given policy (sometimes purposely vague to allow flexibility) could take up much more time than necessary. In addition, incidents, such as a task completed on time at great efforts—rejected by the administrative system, or an important trip delayed because one signature was missing on a piece of paper, did not help professional staff morale either.

To come up with an answer to the problem, I first took an inventory of all administrative actions taking place in the Research and Development laboratories. Each similar action could require different levels of approval. For example, a Purchase Requisition, depending on the Dollar amount. Then, I identified the documents or cover sheets actually receiving the approval or authorization signatures. Next, I classified the documents into seven groups, and the management authorizations into four organization levels.

Finally, I prepared a chart (six typewritten pages) indicating the level and sequence of approval required for each administrative action.

CONCLUSION

My approval chart was so much welcomed by both administrative and technical staffs, that I supplied departments with blank sheets, preprinted in the chart format. Each department entered on its approval chart the most frequent administrative actions taking place, and the names involved in the authorization process. Copies of the chart were distributed to all department personnel. The only investment required was a small printing order, which certainly makes this case a "no cost" improvement.

The following should not be taken as an expression of bitterness. People engaged in productivity improvement work get paid for what they are doing, and the main professional satisfaction comes from a job well done.

How often do people engaged in productivity improvement work receive verbal thanks? From top management, sometimes. From the workers, rarely. In this case, the simplification of burdensome chores was so great, that it did happen.

PRODUCTIVITY IMPROVEMENT CASE HISTORY

EQUIPMENT

SUMMARY:
Building a simple piece of test equipment was a saving, but allowed costly challenges of product quality.   Purchasing an industry standard stopped the problem.

SETTING: Small company, high volume producer of electronic components.

NOTE: This case history was partially described in my lecture titled "PRODUCTIVITY: OUTPUTS AND OUTPUT FACTORS."

At the time when most television sets and components sold in the United States were made here, this small company was the second largest manufacturer of "deflection" components for television cathode ray tubes. (Such components and associated circuits make the electron beam sweep the face of the tube, to form the image.) The relatively simple piece of laboratory equipment used to test the electrical characteristics of such components is called an "impedance bridge."

In the early days of the company, its engineers had built an impedance bridge, which worked well. However, there was no certification or proof that it was really accurate, within accepted industry measurement standards. This fact was exploited by unscrupulous company customers. In a volatile market, television manufacturers would place big orders for components. Then, if sales did not meet expectations, they would return a shipment, stating that the components did not meet specifications.

The company was manufacturing many types of components, some specifically designed for the customer. A returned shipment meant either a cash flow problem, until it was sold to another customer, or a loss, because other customers could not use the components.

A moderately priced impedance bridge, made by the leading U.S. electronic test equipment manufacturer, was recognized world wide as a laboratory standard. I had used it since "Electrical Measurements 101," in France, and in every engineering department I had been associated with. Of course, I recommended its purchase.

The test equipment purchase was well publicized by the company president and the sales people. Some customers sent an engineer to look at it, watch a demonstration on the components they were buying.

CONCLUSION

From that time on, the company had no more problems with customers claiming low quality shipments.

PRODUCTIVITY IMPROVEMENT CASE HISTORY

PRODUCTION ENGINEERING

SUMMARY:
Setup time for production machines reduced from several days to several minutes. Exploration of basic theory provided a method, which turned out to be a first for the industry.

SETTING: Small company, high volume producer of electronic components.

Although a small company, this was the second largest U.S. manufacturer of high voltage transformers for television sets. The high voltage coil in such a transformer (producing some 20,000 volts) is a subject of wonder: The coil, made up of several thousand turns of hair-sized wire, has a cross section shape of about one eight of an inch wide, by one inch high, and must hold up by itself before being assembled and impregnated with wax. The coils are produced on high precision, high speed "honeycomb" winding machines. The secret—why the coil holds up—is that instead of laying one turn of wire next to the other, like sewing thread on a spool, the wire is moved back and forth along the width of the coil, thus securing the wire wound during preceding turns. The lateral movement of the wound wire is determined by a set of gears connected to the winding machine rotating drive shaft. If the wire guiding pattern is not perfect, the coil will collapse before its buildup is completed. Looking at a finished coil shows a honeycomb pattern, a basic mechanical principle for light weight and sturdy construction.

Determining the proper wire guiding pattern for a given coil shape and wire size, then the right set of multiple gears, was a difficult trial and error process, complicated by the fact that gears come only with a "whole" number of teeth. Whenever a new type of transformer went into production, the production manager spent days figuring out a proper machine setup. Usually, he had to come in week ends to work out the problem without interruption.

While I had never even come close to such a machine before, the company chief engineer asked me to give a try at figuring out a better way. He had been working on the problem for some time, and handed me all his documentation: The one and only study on the subject, published by an engineering journal.

It took me several days to understand the study. Then, I realized that what I had to do to design a machine setup was to solve several complicated equations, then test if the answers fit another equation. The process worked, except that it was as time consuming as the trial and error method.

Today, the next step would have been to have a computer program written, then to use a few minutes of computer time when a new transformer design went into production. But this was "before computers."

While doing repetitive engineering work, I could

never see spending time on computation, even with a slide rule. Whenever possible, I used "nomographs," a graphic method to solve equations. A nomograph is a chart made up of several scales. Bouncing a line from one scale to another provides the answers to the equation. If a nomograph was not available for a given type of repetitive problem, I designed my own.

To solve the winding machine setup problem, I designed a nomograph—only to find out that the accuracy afforded by regular size (8 1/2 x 11) chart paper was far from sufficient. On that basis, I ordered the largest size illustration board available, and paper to match.

When I was finished with the nomograph, a few minutes before lunch time, I asked the production manager to give me a coil winding specification, without the machine setup. By noon, I had the machine setup specification, which matched exactly the one used in the factory. However, we did not leave for lunch until the production manager had me repeat the problem solving procedure enough times to assure himself that it worked. It did.

CONCLUSION

The only problem with my nomograph was its size: It was either covering a desk, or hanging on the wall. During a sales call, the president of the largest U.S. coil winding machine manufacturing company noticed the nomograph. He turned buyer, trying to convince the president of the electronic components company to sell it to him: No other transformer manufacturer in the United States had ever solved that production engineering productivity problem.

NOTE ON PERSISTENT PRODUCTIVITY PROBLEMS

A SUGGESTED COURSE OF ACTION

The production engineering—machine setup—case history suggests a course of action for similar situations:

(1) Be persistent in pursuing a solution.

(2) Be open-minded as to the method used, or the person capable of finding a solution.

For example, I have seen many instances of "computer system problems" laying dormant in an EDP department for years. Operating departments having no choice, but deal with the company EDP department, would do nothing, but complain, and suffer. Some outspoken employees would suggest that it is time to replace the EDP department manager.

A open-minded study proved that EDP personnel could not solve the productivity problems, because the real source of the problems was not in the EDP department, not with the computer systems. The computer systems showed only a reflection of the problems.

In preceding lectures, I have emphasized that a "computer" system is only one element of a broader concept "system." In the productivity problem cases referred to here, solving the broad system problems first, allowed the EDP department to supply satisfactory solutions to the operating departments.

A new approach, a fresh look at a productivity problem experienced for years—may solve it.

PRODUCTIVITY IMPROVEMENT CASE HISTORY

MANAGEMENT SYSTEM

SUMMARY:
Timely financial reports problem. My analysis indicated that it was really a backlog problem. Introduction of formal task planning and scheduling solved it.

SETTING: City government.

In most city departments, personnel interested in using financial reports considered what came out from EDP as being of little value. The main reason was lack of timeliness. For example, "July" reports often came out as late as the end of January. During the balance of the year, a two or three months delay was the norm. Then, the report contents were of questionable value: Activity taking place during a given month may show up in a report dated several months later. Thus, a department head could never be sure if rates of department expenditures were in line with the budget. However, the final reports for a fiscal year did reflect accurately what took place during the whole year, and, with the usual adjustments, were accepted by the outside auditors.

The worst time of the year was the beginning of a fiscal year (starting July 1), when it was necessary to close one fiscal year and start a new one—in principle at the same time—on the basis of a new budget adopted in the very last days of June. In the meantime, out of the EDP systems, employees and vendors had to be paid without delay.

> Another bad time was the end of the calendar year, requiring income tax processing. EDP employees were afraid to get into an elevator, where they could be asked "where is my W-2?"

The generation of accounting data did not stop on June 30th, but the computer systems were not ready to process it for months, thus accumulating a huge backlog. The backlog of data contained errors, then corrections to errors. Later on, processing one correction in the wrong computer system sequence could generate several hundred new errors, requiring more correction work, and so on. Eventually, with much hard work and overtime, all the processing would get done, but always late.

When I started studying this situation, I identified the main causes of the problem:

(1) Tradition. For example, the accounting group in a given department knew that it takes two months to prepare certain fiscal year end adjustments. The task would always start towards the end of June, although much of it could have been done before. Then, the ad-

justments had to be reviewed by central accounting before being processed by EDP. Then, computer processing indicated some errors in the adjustments, requiring corrections, etc.

(2) Decentralized accounting. Central accounting received accounting data from many departments. Adjustments were prepared by departments on the basis of data printed in the EDP reports. The result of any delay taking place within such a circular flow of data is obviously a general system delay.

(3) Multiple changes in the EDP systems. This could be the subject for several case histories on computer systems. Anyway, it caused delays.

(4) The size and complexity of the organization involved in the financial reporting process. One financial report was the end result of many tasks performed by many groups, organizationally independent from each other.

(5) Complexity of the financial EDP systems. Reporting requirements for municipal finance are much more complex than for private business. If such requirements could have been met with much less complex systems is another story. Regardless, changing systems is not necessarily a sure or practical way to correct productivity problems experienced with a current system.

(6) In practical terms, although from a point of view rather new for the environment, my analysis of the situation was that we had a production process made up of a very high volume of data moving in a complex pattern through a great number of organizational units. While the task performed by one unit was well coordi-

nated with the next unit, there was no overall coordination—no planning. For example, to start the financial reporting for a new fiscal year, I identified thirty four (34) specific tasks which had to be completed in one (1) given sequence—by EDP, central accounting, and most city departments. However, while all concerned knew exactly what had to be done, there was no overall plan to do it.

SOLUTION

My recommendation to solve the problem had nothing to do with the technical aspects of accounting or computer systems. It was a "no cost" productivity improvement, simply:

> Establish formal planning and scheduling for all manual and computer processing of financial data.

To support my thesis and the feasibility of the solution, I indicated that paychecks are processed on a timely basis. This was accomplished through "cutoff dates" for the manual and computer processing of payroll data—which is a form of planning and scheduling.

CONCLUSION

My task planning and scheduling concept was implemented for the fiscal year closing and opening process. It made everybody's work easier, and it did improve greatly the release date and contents of the "July" financial reports. However, the results were not good enough, and the timeliness of the other monthly reports still left much to be desired.

Through more study, I proved that the "July" and other months' timeliness problems are not separate, but rather one and the same problem. For example, a backlog of accounting adjustments allowed to accumulate all the way to the end of the fiscal year is bound to make the year end closing tasks more difficult and lengthy, thus delaying "June" as well as "July" reports. Similar reasoning, with many more examples, could be extended to any accounting month.

Eventually, a monthly schedule for the completion and transmittal of all tasks pertaining to financial data was adopted. Results:

> For the first time, comprehensive "July" reports were released during the third week of August. From then on, monthly reports came out within one or two weeks following the end of the month.

NOTE ON BACKLOG PROBLEM SITUATIONS

MANAGEMENT SYSTEMS IMPLICATION

The preceding case history proves that backlog problem situations, although established for years, can be successfully resolved.

Backlog is a problem inflicted on society by both private and public service organizations. There is no justification for perennial backlog situations. The time required to perform a given task is the same, whether the work is performed on a current basis—or a long time later.

An all too frequent illustration of the problem has to do with the administration of justice. For example, by the time a child injury case is decided, the child is usually grown up.

Management systems (in the broadest context of the

word "system") are usually at fault.

The answers to the backlog problems are not necessarily simple, but the methodology to follow is the same as for any productivity problem—because backlog is a sure sign of a productivity problem.

How to attack a productivity problem has been treated in the preceding lectures. A condensed summary is:

(1) A commitment from "management" or "government" to solve the problem.

(2) Development of a program, a plan of action.

(3) Persistent program implementation.

PRODUCTIVITY IMPROVEMENT CASE HISTORY

OFFICE PROCEDURE

SUMMARY:
A classic procedure streamlining exercise provided "no cost" improvement: It reduced eleven (11) forms, ledgers and records to one (1) form, solved a six-month processing backlog problem, and allowed the same office staff to handle a workload increase of 100%.

SETTING: City government.

Under a mandatory garbage collection ordinance, the city "scavenger company," a private concern, picks up garbage, regardless if the property owner pays for the service or not. If the property owner does not pay, the scavenger company bills the city, who pays, then starts collection proceedings against the property owner.

I was called in because the paperwork backlog in the city's mandatory garbage office was estimated at six months, and mounting.

I found a situation of strained working relationship between city and scavenger company personnel, and irate citizens complaining about double billing, or unjustified administrative penalties. Searching for documents to support the validity of an account could take hours, or was fruitless. At least half the office personnel appeared to spend most of their time answering complaints, and searching through files.

In the city mandatory garbage office, the supervisor and two employees were accountants. Naturally, they had to set up payable and receivable (manual) accounting systems. They did not believe that all the mandatory garbage accounting information could be found in the city's computerized accounting systems. It is true that the city's accounting systems are rather complex, and mandatory garbage office accountants receiving partial information only from various city accounting sections felt that a comprehensive mandatory garbage accounting system was necessary, for the sake of proper accounting practices, and also to prepare various reports required by city management—always on short notice.

I showed the mandatory garbage office accountants how to find their way through the city accounting systems, and how to correlate the information to fit their needs. In the process, they discovered useful summarizing features in the computer systems, and were finally convinced to abandon their manual ledgers.

In studying the multiplicity of forms and ledgers prepared either for a given step in the collection procedure, or to set up a record, I came to the conclusion that with two additional parts incorporated in the mandatory garbage invoice form—the initial document sent by the scavenger company to the city—not only would all other paperwork and record needs be fulfilled, but the procedure would be simplified, and subject to less errors resulting from copying the same information over several times. The city mandatory garbage office personnel agreed that my proposal could work, if it was possible to produce a new invoice form, satisfying both city and scavenger company requirements.

I had no qualms about promising the scavenger company a new invoice form much easier to prepare, and incorporating any new feature they wished to have: Trying to produce one invoice myself— confirmed my impression that the form had never been really designed for easy typing and preparation.

City urgency for solving the mounting backlog problem permitted me to cut through much red tape in getting legal and other administrative matters settled. Within a couple of months, the new "one-form" procedure was started.

CONCLUSION

The scavenger company was so well satisfied with the improvements resulting from the new procedure, both in its own office and in relation to the city, that it assumed all printing costs for the new invoice form.

City mandatory garbage office personnel had a big job reorganizing their files and catching up with the backlog. Then, the work pace began to drop. By the time consideration was given to transfer out surplus personnel, an increase in city garbage collection fees doubled the number of delinquencies, thus doubling the office workload.

With the new procedure well established, no
new personnel had to be added, and no overtime
was required to handle the 100% increase in office workload.

PRODUCTIVITY IMPROVEMENT CASE HISTORY

EDP PROJECT

SUMMARY:
Two years of low-key EDP system work had offered no alternative to an accounting bottleneck problem. Effective computer project leadership, and active participation from the best EDP and accounting talent available provided the answers. The improvement provided timely accounting statements, saved overtime, and established budget savings amounting to five (5) accounting positions.

SETTING: City government.

BACKGROUND—MUNICIPAL GOVERNMENT ACCOUNTING

A sizable segment of a city budget is assigned to public works and other projects. Financial management of such projects is difficult, because project accounting in a municipal government is a very complicated process. Some of the reasons are stated below.

Both city project work, and project accounting are performed by many departments. Each project performing department uses materials, either purchased for the project, or coming out from central city stores. Some work is performed by outside contractors. City personnel may work on one or several different projects during the same day. Each funding agency (city, state, or federal) has different accounting requirements. One project may have several funding sources with different contractual specifications. For example, allowable overhead rates for the same employee, working on the same state financed project, are different—depending if the work is performed in a sewer, or above ground level. Then, there is the problem of which funding may or may not be carried forward from one fiscal year to the next.

In short, if private business complains about the complications of work financed by one government agency, imagine the complications when one government agency does work financed by several government agencies.

CASE HISTORY

One group of five (5) accountants, a unit of the central city accounting department, was working full time on project accounting. The group maintained ledger cards for several hundred projects, prepared interdepartmental billings, posted all project expenditures and encumbrances (purchasing commitments), figured and billed labor overhead charges, maintained various records, etc.

One built-in problem was that the financial condition of any project, as reflected in city monthly statements, was off by several months, depending on how long it took for documents to come through city project accounting, and other offices. For example, interdepartmental billing for work performed through the end of a given month could not, at best, be entered before the following accounting month.

The city project accounting group, located in one big office, processed and filed an enormous amount of paperwork. Although the group was made up of competent and dedicated individuals, many times during the year, the workload was too much, requiring overtime to catch up with the processing delays.

I became intrigued with this bottleneck situation when I was asked to improve one obvious source of delays in project accounting: The interdepartmental billing procedures.

I found that most of the data coming through the project accounting group (to be worked on, or with) could be found in the city computerized accounting systems, either before, or after work done by the group. I had no doubt that the data processed manually by project accounting could be processed by computer. For other data manually generated by project accounting there was more of a problem, but solutions appeared possible.

I proposed to computerize all the work done by project accounting—only to learn that such a project had been going on "secretly" in the EDP department, for the past two years. Reason for the secrecy was to prevent personnel from wondering about the possibility of jobs being eliminated. The project had a low priority in EDP, and no significant results had been achieved.

I felt that the secrecy approach was wrong, because (1) all project accounting personnel had civil service tenure, and (2) the greatest expertise and experience on the subject was in that group. I also saw no reason for that bottleneck (none of the group's doing) to go on for ever. I started discussing a few ideas with the group supervisor, and received excellent cooperation. A major improvement in the city's project accounting statements was a powerful argument, and pretty soon my computerization project was under way.

Implementing the new concept was no easy task. However, on the accounting side, personnel who knew the most about the principles, details and problems of project accounting gave me all the information I needed. On the EDP side, one of the sharpest programmer I have ever known was assigned to work for me.

No new computer system or subsystem was designed. My idea was to modify existing programs, to perform automatically the processing done manually, since the project accounting data came from the computer systems, and was eventually fed back into the systems.

After the first tests, my programmer reported bad news: The unforgiving computer had discovered a flaw in one modified program logic. For the next few days, I worked full time on computer program logic. I found an answer, and it worked.

CONCLUSION

This was an important change in city administrative

concepts, because it meant a new way to account for a large percentage of the city's budget, funded for the most part by other government agencies. It took about six months for all the accounting and computer "bugs" to show up. All were corrected.

With regard to the five accountants whose functions were eliminated, one decided to take a job closer to home, and four transferred to other positions in the city. In two cases, increased opportunity and employee capability led to promotions.

With all interdepartmental billing done automatically during the daily computer processing of expenditures, the city had now meaningful and timely project accounting reports—and a budget saving of five (5) employees.

PRODUCTIVITY IMPROVEMENT CASE HISTORY

MANUFACTURING

SUMMARY:
Downtime in the production of high priced electronic test equipment had created a serious cash flow problem. A different organization concept, and a new production planning and control system were the solution.

SETTING: Medium size company, leader in its field.

The company president took me to one big storage room in the factory. Benches and shelves were piled high with electronic test equipment units in various stages of completion. The president quoted an astronomical figure, approximating the sales amount tied up in that room. Then, he expressed the most frustrating aspect of this situation: Completion of test equipment units sold for several thousand Dollars each, was held up because a one-Dollar component was not available.

The president did not tell me, but I learned later that the bank had just refused to increase the company's line of credit. The company was in financial trouble.

The very modern factory included a number of production departments, starting with metal working, through final calibration. Many components, including electrical meters, were built in the factory. The company also sold electrical meters to other equipment manufacturers, and to electronic parts dealers.

The electrical meter manufacturing in the company could be described as high-volume assembly line production, while the test equipment manufacturing was a short-run batch production. All the company production was headed by one manager, who had moved up in the company through the meter manufacturing. This point is relevant, because the meter side of the business was a beautiful model of smooth production. The production manager probably preferred managing meter manufacturing over other activities, and he was good at it.

My first reaction was, of course, to evaluate the production planning and control system. There was none, in the usual sense. Instead, four production planning technicians, reporting to the production manager, were supposed to follow through each batch of equipment manufactured, from initial purchasing requests through work orders, and successive stages of completion. Responsibility between planning technicians was divided along product lines.

"Hunters" was the nickname given the production technicians, because they were not supposed to sit at their desks (located in several areas of the factory), but rather to "hunt" all over the factory after the work under their responsibility, making sure that it gets done.

The problem with such an organization was, that while purchasing and production departments were

aware of current requirements, they had no comprehensive visibility of all requirements anticipated within
the next few months.

Purchasing and other departments were managed
by "working supervisors" who had no inclination, or
personnel, to engage in real planning. The most of
whatever planning performed took place in the purchasing department. However, in consolidating and
preparing purchase orders for the several hundred
parts and components required to produce each test
equipment model—it was easy to make one omission.
Two months later, an assembly department would
complete the work required for one batch in production—except for the missing component, and would
send the whole batch to the storage room, while the
purchasing department went into crisis status.

I proposed organization changes, as follows:

(1) The electrical meter manufacturing, not affected
    by the production downtime problem. would be
    left   alone. Changes applied to the electronic test
    equipment manufacturing only.

(2) The work principle of planning technicians phys-
    ically following production through the factory
    would be abandoned.

(3) The planning technicians would work in one cen-
    tral office, following the production process on
    wall planning displays.

(4) The new production planning and control system
    would be based on a single document, a multiple

part form. Each document would describe the materials and work required to complete one manufacturing step, for one equipment model. One document copy would be used to set up the planning display, while other copies forwarded to purchasing and production departments would initiate their own planning, and further work actions.

(5) The "feedback" of document copies, returned from purchasing and production departments, would be used to update the wall planning displays, thus providing central visibility and control for the whole test equipment manufacturing process.

(6) The new organization concept required no additional personnel. It did require a production planning and control system to be designed, and adequate office space to be set up.

The company president accepted my proposal, providing I would design and install the new system. The production manager was more difficult to convince. He was from the old school of foremen, suspicious of any activity not directly related to the actual work do be done. However, once the system project was started, he gave me full cooperation, and saw to it that the production technicians gave me full cooperation too. The purchasing and production departments supervisors welcomed the project, and helped me out.

Training the production technicians was about the most difficult part of installing the new production planning and control system. The technicians' new work pattern was completely different from what they had been doing for years. However, after some initial resistance to the change, things worked out.

CONCLUSION

Converting all the production in process to the new system would have been too much work. The new system was implemented as new production orders were started. Work flow in purchasing and in the production departments became smoother.

The manufacturing downtime problem was solved.

PRODUCTIVITY IMPROVEMENT CASE HISTORY

CORPORATE POLICY

SUMMARY:
Projects delayed or stalled in a large Research and Development organization. A change in corporate policy solved the problem. Additional improvement benefits were gained.

SETTING: Large aerospace corporation, at the time, recognized U.S. leader in electronics.

NOTE: This case history was described shortly in my lecture titled "PRODUCTIVITY: THE ELUSIVE GOLD MINE."

I worked on that project together with the corporate Purchasing Manager. He was trying to improve the productivity of his department, made up of some 250 employees.

I was trying to solve a frustrating productivity problem in the company's Research and Development Laboratories, an organization made up of several thousand engineers and scientists, plus supporting personnel.

The Laboratories' problem was that important, critical projects—were delayed, or stalled—because of delays in the procurement of urgently needed parts, or other small items.

A very large organization does require many fiscal and management controls. The medium to carry out such controls is paperwork. Everybody is aware that paperwork is usually slow, and costly to process. But how costly is often underestimated. At the time, this was the mid-fifties, the Purchasing Manager calculated that processing one purchase order meant a company cost of over $8!

In the Laboratories, while parts and materials needed for Research and Development projects were requested according to well planned schedules, it was not always possible to figure out, in advance, how many parts will be destroyed during testing, or even what will be needed during state-of-the-art research work.

One especially frustrating aspect of the problem was—that a part urgently needed may cost a few Dollars, or even a few Cents—much less than the cost of the paperwork to purchase it—and that further work had to be delayed—while waiting for a long administrative and management approval process to take place.

The answer to such a problem may seem obvious, but anyone experienced with very large organizations will appreciate that it is not always that simple to provide a solution—when, as this was the case, it required changing an established corporate management policy.

The policy was that all purchasing actions had to be channelled through the Purchasing department.

Under the changed policy, the Laboratories' departments were given petty cash funds, and allowed to make, directly, purchases up to an adequate Dollar amount.

Each department had a "property man" taking care of test equipment, materials and supplies. When more electronic components were urgently needed, the property man, following a simple departmental purchasing procedure, would drive to the nearest wholesale, or even retail store where the components were available.

Within a couple of hours, the purchase was delivered directly to the engineers who had made the request, thus avoiding work delays.

CONCLUSION

The frustrating stalled projects—work delays problem in the Research and Development Laboratories was solved.

In the Purchasing department, the change in management policy resulted in a decrease in the number of purchase orders issued, as well as in the paperwork, and other associated purchasing and handling tasks.

Considering the size of the corporation, the few Dollars required to set up the petty cash funds did not count.

> This significant productivity improvement was accomplished—at no cost to the corporation.

ADDENDUM

COMPLAINT IN LINGERIE

SUMMARY:
A money loosing transaction yields long range profits, and helps executive training.

SETTING: Major retail stores chain.

I had nothing to do with this case. I am relating it because:

(1) A person concerned with productivity improvement management should be "tuned in" to any—positive or negative—productivity case. The lesson learned can be useful.

(2) "Services" is now the major sector of the U.S. economy. The retail business is part of it.

(3) The customer concept is not limited to the retail trade. Most work activities involve a "customer."

That friend of mine is a retired high level department store executive. Around 1950, she was in management training in the main store of a retail chain. This included spending a few weeks on the sales floor of every department. During that time, she had a "tutor," a senior executive managing her training.

On that day, she was selling in the lingerie department. An old lady walks in, takes out a pair of "bloomers" from a bag, complains that she is not satisfied with that purchase, and demands a refund.

This type of long undergarment had not been manufactured for about thirty years, and my friend started to put up a fuss. Fortunately, her tutor happened to walk by, and motioned to her to come over, immediately. Between his teeth, he said "give her a credit, with a smile! I'll explain later."

After the customer left, he explained that this is a rich old lady, charging on the average $500 per month (a sizable amount for 1950). Refusing to take back the bloomers would have resulted in the loss of a valuable customer.

CONCLUSION

A person experienced in productivity improvement management tends to evaluate the productivity of any business situation. In the retail business, one often encounters a dismal, deteriorating attitude, which must be blamed on management—failing to keep good sales employees, or to properly train new ones.

Not satisfying customers is a productivity problem leading to business failure.

The problem was well summarized by Cyril Magnin, retired Chief Executive Officer of the J. Magnin retail stores chain. Interviewed when the stores closed to go into bankruptcy, a few years after the chain had been sold to a conglomerate, he stated:

"We were customer oriented. The people who bought us out did not maintain that policy."

Having "customers" is not exclusive to the retail business. Being "customer oriented" is, for most work activities, a major, positive productivity factor.

ACKNOWLEDGMENTS

My sincere thanks for permission to reproduce excerpts of referenced material to the following:

National Bureau of Economic Research. "Productivity Trends in the United States" by John W. Kendrick, 1961.

W.H. Freeman and Company, Publishers. "The Service Sector of the U.S. Economy" by Eli Ginzberg and George J. Vojta. Copyright (c) 1981 by Scientific American, Inc. All rights reserved.

California Alumni Association. "An Interview with Joel Hildebrand" by Timothy Pfaff, California Monthly, October 1981.

American Institute of Industrial Engineers. Excerpts from Industrial Engineering magazine, March 1978, Gerald Nadler article. Copyright Institute of Industrial Engineers, 25 Technology Park/Atlanta, Norcross, GA 30092.

Forbes Inc. "Rising Son," Forbes, February 18, 1980. "Those Simple Barefoot Boys From Iowa Beef," Forbes, June 22, 1981. "Trends—More For Less," Forbes, January 2, 1984.

Dr. Jeremy Bernstein and Basic Books, Inc. "EXPERIENCING SCIENCE" by Jeremy Bernstein, New York 1978. Material was originally published in The New Yorker, October 20, 1975, under the title "PROFILES—PHYSICIST, I.I. RABI."

Columbia University Press. "Productivity Improvement" by Donald C. Burnham. Copyright 1973 by Carnegie-Mellon University.

American Management Association, Inc. "The Management Evolution" by Lawrence A. Appley, 1963.

LIST OF FIGURES AND TABLES

FIGURES

TABLES

INDEX

NOTE

The word "productivity" has been omitted from many index entries, since the entire text relates to productivity.

ORDER FORM   To: CALIFORNIA MANAGEMENT PRESS
Please mail with your   236 West Portal Avenue, Suite 114
check. Thank you.   San Francisco, CA 94127-1423

Please send _____ PRODUCTIVITY IMPROVEMENT MANAGEMENT book(s)
priced $18.00 plus $2.00 for shipping/handling.
In California add sales tax: 6% $1.08 - 6.5% $1.17 - 7% $1.26.

$ _____ check enclosed.

        Name _____

        Title _____

        Affiliation _____

        Address _____

        City, State, ZIP _____

"Every management professional can
benefit from reading this book."